Advanc

Sailing the Mystery

"Welcome aboard this wondrous sailing adventure, inspired by the spirit of Ed Merck's quest on the sea of his third age. Journey with him across these pages as he explores the uncharted waters of his life with insight, courage and wisdom. Sailing the Mystery offers you a beautiful map to sail into the mystery of your own life."

Alan O'Hare
Director, Life Story Theatre
Author, *Love Mary B: A Teacher's Life*

"Sailing the Mystery is a powerful and thoughtful book. We learn from Ed's experience that where we are heading isn't a place, but a process. This necessitates leaning into our own discomfort as we confront our old stories and write new ones, all in the course of connecting with our authentic self. The journey of aging can be fraught with doubts and fears, but is also empowering and exhilarating. This book is a good lesson for us all."

Dorian Mintzer, Ph.D.
Co-author, *The Couple's Retirement
Puzzle: 10 Must-Have Conversations for
Transitioning to the Second Half of Life.*

"Sailing the Mystery describes one man's response to the central question that exists in all humans—what does life mean to me? We are compelled—beyond logic—to respond to the unrelenting 'call' of something bigger than us. Ed Merck's journey is to follow that scary, irresistible urge, which he does with unmistakable, and unyielding, courage."

Dr. David Berceli
Founder and CEO of
Trauma Recovery Services

Sailing the Mystery

My Journey into Life's Remaining Chapters

by Ed Merck

The passage excerpted from the poem "Bouyancy" on
page vi is used with permission from Coleman Barks and
Maypop Press.

Produced by:

FriesenPress
Suite 300 – 852 Fort Street
Victoria, BC, Canada V8W 1H8

www.friesenpress.com

Distributed to the trade by The Ingram Book Company

Table of Contents

Buoyancy*

So the sea-journey goes on, and who knows where!
Just to be held by the ocean is the best luck
we could have. It's a total waking up!

Why should we grieve that we've been sleeping?
It doesn't matter how long we've been unconscious.

We're groggy, but let the guilt go.
Feel the motions of tenderness
around you, the buoyancy.

RUMI

Passage excerpted from the poem "Buoyancy" as published in "The Essential Rumi," with permission from Coleman Barks and Maypop Books.

INTRODUCTION

In what seemed like an instant, I retired from full-time work, my marriage unraveled, and my son went off to college. Yikes—I didn't know who I was anymore. It felt like everything had been taken away—or worse, that I had bet my life on a good hand, and lost.

This much was clear: I was done living out our culture's stock formulas for fulfillment. Instead, I felt a determination within to discover my own version of what it meant to welcome in the final chapters with vitality and purpose. I could hear the Universe speaking to me: *feel the exhilaration that comes from embracing the implicit danger of the unknown.* Yet I had only the slightest awareness of how to construct such a reality.

So, I went to the sea to find myself, again. Somehow, down deep, I knew that only a full immersion into the energy of the ocean would bring me home to my authentic self. And I knew that arriving at my deathbed without having at least attempted my dream of long-distance sailing was unacceptable, even if I ended up not liking it. In my view, the only failure would be not having tried.

Throughout my journey I relied on the complex and hard-to-define essence of *spirit*. When I trusted it, and allowed it to be present in my life, it would anchor and guide me. I have learned that what my head tells me is only one source of knowledge, and often not the most reliable.

I had no idea how this year of intense transition and personal growth would evolve when I set sail. At times it was scary, especially when I realized there wasn't even a destination to be had, merely an unfolding process. For sure, there were plenty of risks, like abruptly stopping work, leaving my beloved house and community behind, sailing the ocean while putting my life and the lives of others on the line, and loving another imperfect being. All that in pursuit of a more in-depth, engaged life.

I sailed into the emptiness, only to discover that life is not about resolution; we just keep adding capacity to engage more of the mystery. And *that* is the miracle.

Please, come join me on my journey.

Ed Merck, October 2012

A NOTE TO READERS

"Memoir is how one remembers one's own life," says Gore Vidal. In writing *Sailing the Mystery,* I adhered to that description with as much veracity as seemed prudent.

Yet a strict obedience to fact is not always the most effective means of communicating "essence." Portraying the deeply emotional, or even spiritual heart of a memory is sometimes at odds with a doggedly factual representation. For me, this was particularly the case when unfolding the relationship with my then-partner, Samantha. To better get at the "truth" of my connection to her, and its healing effect on me, I occasionally created and/or embellished upon the literal story in order to more cogently represent the spirit of my life challenges and glories. All other aspects of this book are exact remembrances of my life here on planet earth.

For the sake of privacy, I have changed most names in *Sailing the Mystery,* making exceptions only for those who requested use of their common names.

Foster House—Exterior

1
Letting Go

Spring 2009

Walking through the vacant rooms, I am consumed by memories—the friends who visited me, the lovers who slept with me, the son who bonded with me, the birds that sang to me, and oh, so much more.

The imperative of letting go taunts me. I need to move ahead, but instead I find myself holding on to what feels familiar. Emotions and rationality collide. I am lost in a tidal wave of hurt and loss, while my head says *Enough, let's move it on out already.*

This going from living on the land to living on the sea seems essential, even if I'm not sure of all the reasons why, and even if it scares the hell out of me. Only the ocean—that great metaphorical model of impermanence and emptiness—can offer me the needed support in this life transition. I know this deep in my gut.

The phone rings on the lone remaining hall table. It is Garth, my longstanding friend and neighbor.

"Hey bro, can I talk you out of this?" he says, diving right in without a hello. "Like, what the hell are you doing? Are you really going to leave me, your house, your buddies—everything?" He is relentless. "You have no idea what's out there. I haven't always been the best friend, but I am *your* friend." He adds, "Try to find that on the road, jerkhead."

I stumble through a pathetic response and hang up. Garth's words linger, hitting my growing fear of losing all I've worked for over the past forty years. Yet down deep I know that now is the time to uproot and move on.

My house in Foster, Rhode Island and the land it sits on are beautiful and serene. But they no longer call to me. It is as if some vital part of me—my spirit—has already moved on, leaving behind an empty place with haunting memories. Not long ago I truly

Only the ocean—that great metaphorical model of impermanence and emptiness—can offer me the needed support in this life transition.

believed this home would be my final resting place. Instead, it has become like all the others: a temporary stopover point along the route to "somewhere." I created the perfect blue/gray clapboard house in the woods. Yet I've come to see the double edge of such a place that once captured my heart, and now has run its course.

Garth's call caught me by surprise, but his words have a familiar ring. This leave-taking is nothing new. I have forever been a nomad; change must be my soul's mantra. Almost always when landing at what might be a resting place, an inner compulsion told me it was time to seek new challenges. While I haven't liked the disequilibrium that comes from a life in perpetual motion, in hindsight the rewards of discovering new territory have always been worth the pain.

Somehow, though, this transition feels much bigger than the others. Perhaps that's because it requires a leap into a whole new stage of life, *my final third*, which catches me off guard. I'm used to growth spurts coming incrementally, as though they are building on a foundation. In contrast, this one demands a whole-sale shift in focus, even identity. I need to let go of the past, yet moving out of Foster feels like a seismic shift in consciousness, with all its discomfort and chaos. No wonder I fear this change as much as I desire it.

I've spent the last twenty years in and around Providence, Rhode Island, and during this last month the memories have haunted me at every turn. After all, this is the place where my son Evan grew from a baby to a young adult; where my seventeen-year marriage to Catherine blossomed, wilted, and eventually faded; where my forty-year career flourished and ended; where the most meaningful friendships of my life were made, developed, and sustained; and where I too grew up (though some would argue with that conclusion).

I enter Ryan's (our local general store) for what may be the last time. Its smell of coffee, soap powder, and wooden floors makes me think intensely of Evan, now twenty-one. When he was between the ages of two and ten, we would do the weekly shopping together every Saturday morning. Initially facing me in the child seat of the carriage, I was fascinated by his inquisitive and trusting eyes. "Just the boys," we would say to each other with a smile, while exploring our overlapping worlds. Now, in this bittersweet moment, standing amid the produce and fresh fish, I know all too well that these memories will continue to fade, and that the direct experience will never again be available.

Evan was a precocious, blue-eyed, blonde-haired kid who just knew he was smarter than his dad. One Saturday morning on the way home from Ryan's, we were pulled over by a town policewoman for traveling a bit too fast. As the cop approached the car, I tried to cover up my transgression by pretending that she was paying us a friendly call. I didn't want that little three-year-old, still in a car seat, to be one up on his dad, and I *was* trying to set a good example.

"So Dad, where's the fire?" was her opening gambit.

Fighting back my fear of exposure, I handed over my license and registration in as casual a manner as possible, hoping that my status as a local would soften her judgment. She looked in the car, stared at Evan, and somehow—perhaps sensing my discomfort—turned quickly cooperative, waving me off with just a verbal warning.

Convinced that my cover-up (with Evan) had been successful, I drove off feeling relieved that I'd gotten off scot-free. Until a minute later when he leaned over and whispered, "Dad, I don't think we should tell Mom about this one."

"Right," I said, feeling both exposed by Evan, and proud of him. I'd be happy to pay a steep summons, and even endure the policewoman's full repertoire of reprimands, if I could relive that moment…and many others.

These memories, which span half of my adult life, reflect a deep connection to my community. It is my story—a unique tapestry of players, places, things, and other fellow travelers—woven out of our shared histories. Important conversations with friends, challenges at work, and even my labors with the land have helped define me. Disentangling now is nothing short of gut-wrenching, and the closer I come to actually leaving my house and community, the more my longing to hold on intensifies.

I step into the cream-colored bathroom. My eye immediately catches the custom-sized tub which triggers a long-held memory. It's only a thought from the past, but it lives on with its own unique vibration.

Phyllis approached the tub with a terrycloth robe partially draped over her smooth, naked shoulders. "Let me in," she said coyly, dipping a toe into the tepid water. As she did, the robe split, revealing her beautiful silken leg and just a hint of her neatly trimmed flower. Reaching out, I gently pulled her into the tub, allowing her practiced resistance, and my persistent desire, to fuel our passion. Yes, a chapter once lived, that now is ended.

Over the years, plenty of women have roamed the hallways and other rooms of this house. I love the female gender, probably a bit too much. Yet I always seem to go for more than is realistic, wanting a lover, a friend, a soul mate, and a spiritual buddy all in one. Consequently, the women in my life have come and gone, some staying longer than others, some cutting deeper than others. The lessons of love and desire have been numerous, and often painful, but now the universe is coaxing me to let go and move on—alone.

Stumbling into what was my home office, a well-remembered call rings through my memory.

It was Bill, the CFO of a major university. "Ed," he exclaimed, "You guys really hit the jackpot this time. We love this strategic planning software, and so does our president. You made me a hero on my own turf." Another satisfied customer in what began as a modest part-time venture. Within a few short years, my partners and I created the premier financial planning software used in higher education today.

I was a *somebody* in my day. Now, standing in that room with hollowness in my throat, I realize, I'm becoming a *nobody*.

These thoughts scare me. Yet at the same time, my mind dances with pleasurable visions of the future, an imagined time of floating freely on the ocean. Despite my fear of leaving, I am looking forward to living the life of a full-time sailor. This is my chance to be totally immersed in the energy of the sea, something I have looked forward to for most of my adult life.

The phone rings, this time for real. It is my mother, and I immediately hear the concern in her voice.

"So, Binky (my childhood nickname), are you really going to sell your beautiful house and move to a boat?" Her voice is deceptively soft and, to an outsider, empathic. "You've gone from nothing to everything in your life. I am so proud of you." She's said these things before—but then her real reason for the call emerges. "And why would you go off alone? Won't you be lonely?"

I usually write this stuff off as typical motherly concerns. This time, however, she is naming what I have been struggling to avoid: my fear of loneliness.

Ah, that is the dreaded double curse, I think. *Becoming a nobody, and having nobody to share it with.* No wonder leaving is so painful—it's only partially about moving. The real subtext is the inner transformation of Ed.

Like it or not, this is my time to dismantle the identity I spent so many years developing, the one based on external roles in career and parenting. In its place I'm aware of the need to move into a more spiritually-centered form of knowing, one that is inwardly focused. Whoa, did I sign up for this? And if so, why didn't I read the fine print? Maybe the real price of moving to a more authentic life is beyond my means.

"I'll be fine, Mom," I say, hoping it's true. "I'll only know once I do it."

I forge ahead with the task at hand, packing the relics of a life to-date. These aren't just a few holdovers from my five-year stay in Foster. Here in these cobwebbed, dusty, and partially crushed boxes lies the accumulation of sixty-three years

Ah, that is the dreaded double curse. Becoming a nobody, and having nobody to share it with.

of life on planet earth. Even my baby book is present, passed on years earlier from Mother, with first tooth intact.

A handwritten note drops out of a book on its way to a box. It is dated April 28, 1988—written by a prominent mid-western university president, a mentor I held in great esteem at the beginning of my career. I stare at his scratchily penned words.

Ed, Please be assured I would be glad to act as a reference for jobs back East. Please also be assured that we would be delighted if you could overcome your lust for the sea and remain here in the calmer waters of Lake Ontario.

With admiration,

Russ.

The tears flow profusely as questions loom. Was progress in my career worth leaving an established community of engaging and talented colleagues? Would my family have been better off had we stayed? Had I unwittingly and unadvisedly put job and income potential ahead of…everything?

And did I risk never again connecting with so vibrant a mentor? Unfortunately, the answer to this last question is, yes. I took the gamble, and lost. There's never been another boss that I respected and learned as much from. Tears now show me the depth of that regret, still alive today after many years.

So, why move on? Why not bask in the glow of my story, the sense of belonging that I have worked so hard over the years to create? Why not just harvest the low-hanging fruit of my life instead of uprooting it all now and jumping into a sea of change?

I'm tempted to be flip and say something like, "Damned if I know." And the truth is that I don't have a simple answer—or at least a culturally acceptable one. Something fundamental in me has already moved on, I know that. And there is a major

…this is my time to dismantle the identity I spent so many years developing, the one based on external roles in career and parenting. In its place I'm aware of the need to move into a more spiritually-centered form of knowing.

transition within me begging to happen. Maybe the answer is as simple, and profound as: *in order to catch up with my spirit.*

Mine (I think) has already left to go sailing.

Foster House—Interior

2
Showing Up

Finally, I am packed and ready to bid farewell. Everything that is going with me on this leg of the journey has been shoehorned into my Subaru and I've said my goodbyes. The house is now ready for the new owners.

It is a spectacular May morning—crisp, dry, not too hot, not too cold—and all washed with bright-yellow sunlight streaming through the newly leafed-out hardwoods. After a brief visit from my friend Mike, I am at last alone, opening slowly to the reality of this tender moment. The final act has arrived. This is the last time I will plant my feet on the land, feel its energetic pulse, and gaze back at the house I still love. Gosh, the magnificent structure looks so beautiful, regal in its own right, yet fully integrated into the natural landscape. I'm already missing her, and I haven't even left.

Standing there, I remember our first date, way back in 2002. It was the classic love at first sight. Within the first few minutes of walking the periphery, I felt the instant chemistry between us. The trees that covered most of the property were a rich mix of relaxed old hardwoods and younger more recent additions. It was fall, and they were proud to be displaying their truly magnificent blend of reds, greens, yellows—even a few dark purples. Interspersed among the trees were impressive outcroppings of strongly articulated gray-blue ledge, much of it covered with light-green lichen. Mother Nature had done her best work, and I quietly hoped she would pick me as her next beneficiary.

Adding to the skillful mixture of vibrant colors and deep hues was the terrain, interesting mostly for its varied palette. Not a flat surface to be found except for the lovely and vibrantly green meadow, upon which sat the vulnerable, small, tattered wood house. At the extreme end of the property, facing into the forest and high up on a ledge, was a worn and decaying platform. This perch, I speculated, had been built by the former owners to help them connect to the land. It sure felt connected to me as I stood there lost in the moment, drinking in the sweet life-energy of nature's varied ensemble.

Instinctively, I assumed a seated meditation position on the platform and listened. *Wow, what a hot, energetic spot,* I thought. With my eyes closed, I envisioned a circus-like community of beings saying, "Yes, please take me, take us." If the realtor had been present, I would have offered full price for the privilege of immediate access to this treasured platform.

I bought the house that same year—exactly eighteen months before moving in. Located in rural Foster, Rhode Island, it was nestled in a spot where the deer, thankfully, outnumber the humans. A simple cape, this lonely structure had been grossly neglected since its creation twenty-five years earlier. Its few windows were covered with growth from untrimmed bushes and small trees. Paint—whatever was left of it—was in various stages of peeling, and inside the house smelled of dampness, old trash, and well-entrenched mold.

I imagined this time-worn house as a person approximately my age whose prime time had passed, resulting in premature wrinkles, creaky joints, and clogged plumbing. In short, an organic entity on whom the weight of life's responsibilities had seriously taken its toll. But I adored the location, and at that time my spirit was being drawn toward it as much as it is now being pulled away. Besides, I couldn't resist all the potential; I hoped that with a good design team, this tired old house would take on a new, vibrant persona.

It had been two years since my divorce from Catherine, Evan's mother. Her steady, supportive presence would not, regretfully, be available to help me through this project. What I really needed was input from someone who had a refined artistic sense and who would later be my housemate (and lover). Having a few bucks to share in the investment wouldn't have hurt either. But while there was some feminine conceptual influence in the early stages that held the promise of more (or so I thought), by the time I moved in this house had become a home for me alone.

Under my care and direction, the team of designers and builders set out on a year-long project to remake the weary structure into a proud, receptive home. Surfaces were stripped down to the studs in preparation for the addition of many new features like dormers, decks, and additional rooms. Reaching deep into the underbelly, we refreshed electrical and plumbing systems; resurfaced every floor, wall, and ceiling; and added all new lighting and plumbing fixtures. In the end, this wasn't just a makeover. Our team had essentially created a whole new being, one that had stature, integrity, and grace.

Post-renovation, the entire south face of the house, where the sun streamed in during the day, was composed of floor-to-ceiling windows which lit up the space like a grand cathedral. Large bay windows added an interesting asymmetrical visual rhythm. Connecting the structure to the earth was a forty-six-by-twelve foot deck that spanned the entire length, stepping gradually down from the edge of the house to the edge of the land. Inside the natural world continued to dominate, with flooring of rough-finished wide-pine boards, blue Vermont slate, and black-and-white-grained granite sinks hand-picked from the quarry. All was bathed in sunlight and soft incandescent light.

I'll never forget my first evening at the newly remodeled house. It was January, 2004. The land outside was covered with pure virgin snow, and a stunning red fox sat perched atop one of several large granite boulders at the other end of the field.

> *Melodies, harmonies, fugues—anything musical had always been an essential part of my life, the only steady lover I ever really had.*

The woodstove was ablaze, emitting bone-penetrating warmth only possible from wood heat. I sat down in my chair—my nesting place—and what I felt was: *I am finally home. I am safe again.*

I loved all the rooms in this new house: the bedroom, with its huge skylight over the bed for star-gazing; the central bathroom, with full-body step-in tub and beautiful hand-built sinks; the office/guest room, with its Murphy bed; and the living room, built around a large soapstone woodstove with its own large skylight. My favorite room of all was a new addition, the music room.

For me, this was the temple. It was in this room of all pine wood and cathedral ceilings where I worshipped, sometimes alone and sometimes in concert with Evan. Melodies, harmonies, fugues—anything musical had always been an essential part of my life, the only steady lover I ever really had.

Back then I was truly delighted in the way this room held both my strong reverence, and Evan's own growing fondness, for music. It became the space that embraced our mutual passion, and perhaps the deepest bond between us. This love of music had to be carefully wooed, however. I didn't want my adoration of it to swamp his growing affection for it. Of course, in reality, I was hungry for the intimacy that playing music together could offer, and I sensed that he was too.

First there was the prelude, the veiled invitation, neither of us wanting to show too much vulnerability.

"So, Evan, are you up for a few tunes?"

"Yeah, sure, Dad," he said, not looking up from the computer. "Maybe in a bit."

Then there was the main act. Suspended in time and separated from our usual roles as father and adolescent son, we became absorbed in the magic of Renaissance and Baroque wind music—allemandes, sarabandes, minuets, and gigues. Twisting and turning with every subtle nuance, we shaped the music, and our deepening relationship to each other.

Twisting and turning with every subtle nuance, we shaped the music, and our deepening relationship to each other.

All was held visually and acoustically by this beautiful room of windows on three sides, with its rich wood surfaces and vaulted, wood-covered ceiling. In this sacred space we pursued music's muse together.

I snap back to the present—spring, 2009. Can I do this? Can I really walk away from the place that faithfully held and nourished me over the years? Can I leave this behind and risk composing a whole new life, one whose basic contours have only begun to emerge?

True, I have already purchased a sailboat to live on, so there is some certainty as to what I am headed toward. However, the world of living full-time on the water is, to me, anything but familiar territory. Doubts loom heavy about the ultimate usefulness of a floating home. Can I die to this life on land, as I reach forward to a new one on the sea?

Despite the warm emotions I feel for the house, and all the rich experiences it has brought me, it is time to go. I know this, and say it to myself like a mantra amidst the swirling doubt. I'm hoping the inertia of staying is finally being toppled by the need to follow my deeper intention. I can come back to Foster, but at my advancing age, I cannot later rediscover the sea.

Yet I have no idea how to leave in a way that bears a shred of dignity. I feel uncomfortably vulnerable, like having to end a romantic relationship without the benefit of a closing fight, and the heated energy to push me through it.

Then I remember Steve, my friend and the minister of a Unitarian Universalist church I attended sporadically. His unexpected announcement—that he was moving to another church—caught us all by surprise. During his last service, Minister Steve spoke persuasively about how the broader culture was better at starting relationships than finishing them. "We put a lot of care and love into how we begin," he explained, "but typically the exit door comes without the same amount of thoughtfulness. And, more often than not, there is hurt, anger, and even disillusionment that never gets addressed or, much less, resolved."

Can I die to this life on land, as I reach forward to a new one on the sea?

I have to admit, my track record is no exception. How I wish I could redo the final phases of many past and especially intimate relationships. And while my house is a structure, not a person, I nevertheless feel a deep connection to it.

Adding a bit of levity to this otherwise sobering memory, I recall sitting in church at Steve's final service, thinking of the last episode of the TV series MASH. In the end Hawkeye Pierce, (who wore his feelings on his sleeve) and BJ Hunnicutt (who was emotionally introverted) parted company after years of friendship. Try as he might, Hawkeye, who was as effusive in his farewell as he had been in everyday TV episode life, couldn't get BJ to say goodbye. Then Hawkeye, who left first in a helicopter, looked down and saw a huge GOODBYE on the ground below, created by hundreds of leftover toilet paper rolls, with BJ

standing next to the powerful graphic smiling and waving profusely. For me, the message was clear. Personalize your parting
message however you want—just make sure you show up for the
final goodbye.

So, here I am, only a few minutes from that last goodbye,
filled with every icky emotion under the sun, and no helicopter
or toilet paper rolls to offer direction. After all the build up about
dignified goodbyes, I end up engaging in a ritual that neither BJ
nor Hawkeye would have likely considered. In fact, I avoid even
designing a final closure in favor of just listening, tuning in to the
moment, and following its direction.

I sit meditation-style at the edge of the deck, looking out
into the forest, wearing nothing more than blue jeans and a grey
t-shirt. My eyes are closed, my breathing slows, and I feel my
entire being asking for guidance. With each deepening breath
I taste the sweetness of the land. As I further quiet, the pale
notes of paint, wood preservative, and newly cut grass emerge.
Waves of light flow over me as my body softens and my mind
is calmed. After a few minutes in silence, I am moved to chant
"Om," the sound of the universe. And then I find my way into a
deeper silence.

Out of the emptiness emerges a vibrant connection to all
around me—the trees, the birds, the rock, and yes, the house.
It is much more than connecting through a heightened sense of
hearing and seeing. It feels to me as if our spirits are merging.
What better way to part, I think, *than to experience together the
very connection we have nurtured over the past five years—like a
spontaneous and unspoken form of celebration for what we have
created, and now I must leave.* With tears of gratitude in my eyes
I bow in all directions, slowly walk to the car, open the door, get
in, and drive off.

Releasing the Covenant

In saying goodbye,

we honor the connection between us.

Moving into silence to better feel

what we have created together.

Nothing new,

it has been here all along.

What's left is to acknowledge,

bow, and depart.

Binky—a Childhood Force, and with Eyes that Yearn

3

On the Road...to Faith and Belief

No sooner is Foster, Rhode Island, in my rear-view mirror than I start to have memories of other drives, and other times, when life was both sweet and challenging.

Heading down the long wooded driveway to Evan's school, in the autumn of 1996, it was easy to spot my starry-eyed, highly energetic second grader. He and his forty-five other schoolmates were playing basketball as they awaited their rides home. I reached over to open the door while watching him run to the car and then swing himself athletically into the front seat.

"So, what did you learn today?" I asked, swept along by his bright, youthful energy.

"Cool stuff Dad, all about how dolphins make babies."

"Wow, that sounds interesting," I said, beginning to wonder about the topic myself. And then I felt a shot of recognition waking me to the possibility of expanding the theme of dolphin mating into that of the "birds and the bees." For months I had been looking for a hook, so without missing a beat, I let it rip. "Humans are mammals too, Evan. That's how you were made by Mommy and Daddy."

He stares out the window.

"No, I mean it," I said gently, trying to stay on point, "dolphins and humans…"

"No kidding, Dad," he said with a hint of distain, "do you think I don't know that?"

Years later, we were again in the car for what seemed like part two of the same conversation. Evan was a teenager, and I was driving him to high school for the morning drop off. Several days earlier I had engaged in a hastily arranged phone conference that included Evan's girlfriend's mother, Liz, Catherine (my then former wife), and me. The topic? What should we do about our kids' attraction to one another and their impending intimacy?

Catherine, always the tender, practical one, said, "It's inevitable, let's just help them be safe."

Liz, quick on the trigger, countered with, "Over my dead body."

While wondering how I got between these two women, I said to myself, *Oy vey, let them work it out*. Long story short, I was deputized to give Evan the safe-sex speech, and Liz would do the same for her daughter after she (probably) locked her in her room.

"So, Evan," I said, flying down the highway doing sixty plus, "it's wonderful that you and Jennifer are feeling so close lately." Rather than waiting for him to respond I plowed on. "Just in case you choose to move into something deeper, you know, intercourse [I whisper], I need to explain a few precautions for you to take." (*I was wondering why it was easier for me to discuss million dollar deals than to talk about sex with my son.*)

I looked over as he reached into his pocket, pulled out his wallet, and fished around inside. Then, with an air of triumph he held up a prophylactic in purple foil and said, "Dad, I'm way ahead of you." Offering an embarrassed, polite smile as my response, I thought to myself, *Well, first I'm outgunned by two mothers, and now outmaneuvered by my sixteen-year-old son.*

What is it about driving that encourages familiarity? Over the years, many of my most memorable exchanges with people I love have taken place in the "sanctuary" of an automobile. It is difficult for me to imagine talking about sex with my child in any other venue. Equally difficult to imagine are the myriad, and often thorny, conversations with myself, usually in deep reflection over disturbing trends in current events (mine), or those of the past (also mine).

As I head towards Connecticut on this fine spring day in 2009, and begin connecting to the open-endedness of both the highway and my life, there certainly is plenty to reflect on. *This is an exercise in trust that the path before me will organically emerge. It will be a matter of putting one foot in front of the other, without concern for the ultimate direction.* At least that's what I tell myself. But after only an hour on the road, I am already questioning the wisdom of leaving my house and community behind, and whether I have the mettle to pull it off.

Perhaps out of that sense of self-doubt, a long forgotten image emerges in my mind's eye. It is the United States Immigration Report that hung framed on my parent's living room wall. This slightly stained and browning document details when my maternal grandparents arrived at Ellis Island in 1921, after a long and rocky boat ride across the Atlantic from Czechoslovakia.

As I remember my grandmother telling the story in broken English, they arrived with two suitcases, twenty dollars in debt, and scared out of their minds. Their clothes were tattered, neither grandparent had a job waiting for them, and they were hungry. Plus, there was that infant child (my mother), who, according to my grandmother, was a holy terror even back then.

I wonder what it was that made them leave their homeland for a new life, and why they were the only siblings from very large families to do so. More globally, what is it that pushes some of us to nest in one place for most of our lives, while others remain constantly in motion? Sinking deeper into reflection...

am I living a journey similar to that of my grandparents, and is my current anxiety over this separation from the familiar actually helping me appreciate for the first time the depth of their choices, and subsequent struggles? More poignantly, does my current transition into the final third contain within it the shadows of their rocky transition into adulthood? Perhaps there is still something for me to learn from them.

Closer to home, I'm reminded of my brother Tom, who was my roommate in childhood. He has, for the better part of the last forty years lived in the same house, been married to the same woman, had the same job, and eaten lunch at 11:30 each day of the work-week on the same workbench. Yes, forty years. In our mother's address book there is only one entry for him. Her records for me in the same book consist of four pages of crossed out locations and phone numbers. Now she doesn't even know what to put down—a boat? The sea? The universe?

What is it that pushes some of us to nest in one place for most of our lives, while others remain constantly in motion?

Hitting the grooved pavement in the break-down lane brings me abruptly back into the present. More questions shake loose. Have I put too much on the line? Did I overestimate my capacity for moving into the vast unknown?

I sense that I'll have to inhabit a kind of spiritual emptiness before even beginning to know what the hell is going on. Am I ready for this, or is it all just an intellectual construct, the actualization of which I'll fail at miserably? Yes, I can manage anything. Trusting in the future, however—perhaps that is above my pay grade.

Brother Tom—the trip maker in our family—advised me to just kick back, turn on cruise control, and enjoy. If he can do it, certainly I can. Yet, in all fairness to me, on Tom's excursions he always had a place to come back to. His trips were more like vacations *from something*, not a clean break *into nothing*.

I call Tom at midday to check directions—or is it for comfort? He repeats, "Just kick back, turn on the cruise control, and enjoy." It might be worth noting here that my car's cruise control hasn't been working for the past two months, but when I try it now, it snaps right in without protest. A gentle nudge from the universe?

As I engage the repetitiveness of the road, my body softens and my mind begins to slow down. Mile after mile the hypnotic rhythm provides the spaciousness I need to sink deeper into the moment without the benefit—safety, really—of knowing where my life is headed. This is my faith. It has grown over time from the need for certainty, however illusory, to a place of acceptance, knowing that this is just where I need to be even if—perhaps especially if—I can't explain why. And if the road ahead is set with minefields, that doesn't mean I shouldn't be on it. *Just be sensitive to where you put your foot,* I remind myself. *And listen intently. That is all you need to do.*

I know I can manage anything. Trusting in the future, however—perhaps that is above my pay grade.

In one of his monologues on midlife the poet David Whyte says, paraphrasing Dante, "If you wake up in the middle of your life and the way looks wholly dark; be comforted by knowing your eyes will grow accustomed to the darkness." This feels right to me. Despite the abundance of ambiguity, I nevertheless sense that this

My faith has grown over time from the need for certainty—however illusory—to a place of acceptance, knowing that this is just where I need to be even if—perhaps especially if—I can't explain why.

moment is perfect just the way it is. Of course there will be plenty of additional growth along the way. My task now, I say to myself, *is to accept the road I am on, and to see that where I am headed is not a place, merely an unfolding process.*

Underscoring this faith is a core belief I've held since childhood that somewhere, somehow, there is always a "silent hand" at work, a beneficent power higher than myself that is looking out for my best interests. It often hasn't felt that way when I was going through a difficult time, but hindsight always confirmed the rightness of each of my challenges, and the joys that often ensued.

I catch myself sounding Pollyannaish. Not a good place to be according to my overactive mind that demands I use good science to make decisions. Nevertheless, I feel these things in my bones. They are part of my truth.

Back to the road and to hearing my brother's advice: kick back, turn on cruise control, and enjoy.

Out in the World

4
Growing Up Rough

Around the New York/Pennsylvania line, I find myself starting to muse on where my faith has come from. What are the experiences that formed me; that have brought me to this place of trust and inner knowing? How has this sixty-three-year-old man behind the wheel of his beat-up Subaru been shaped into a mature human being, the one now careening at 75mph into the void, and still feeling okay?

Childhood on Long Island, New York wasn't easy. On the surface I was just your average kid engaged in typical activities. I loved to play any kind of ball, enjoyed and excelled in Boy Scouts before they became homophobic and paramilitary, got average grades in an average academic track, had a close circle of guy friends, played the girl scene with typical adolescent fervor and awkwardness, enjoyed the spotlight and the swing that musical performance afforded me, and fought with my parents for freedom of expression.

But scratch the surface a bit and you'd find a kid who often felt out of step with…well, almost everything. I sensed there was a lot more to life than what lay before me. Yet, at the same time, I didn't know where to look for the connections to this felt reality. My teachers didn't provide it. The Catholic Church, which I attended out of family obligation, certainly didn't offer it. And my parents were often a disappointment when it came to reaching beyond the obvious. They meant well and tried very hard, but had a limited repertoire to draw from.

Compounding the problem, I was an unusually bright, sensitive kid who was growing up as a first-generation American in a sterile cultural and intellectual environment. My father, who was an amazing inventor, only made it through eighth grade before having to enter the work-a-day world. *The Daily News,* and not *The New York Times,* was the paper of choice. I was searching for deeper connections to the larger world, but the guideposts were not at all visible to me. Like a stranger in a strange land, I felt alienated from most of the adults in my life—often consumed by an acute sense of loneliness without knowing what to do about it.

It was a hot summer day in 1956 as the six of us packed into the overly tight red and white Buick for an outing at the beach. I looked forward to getting out of the small house that held four boys, a father, and a mother all stacked on top of one another. Mom and Dad had their own bedroom, and the four boys split the other two rooms that were actually more like closets. Imagine the six of us sharing one bathroom in the morning before work and school.

Exacerbating the physical constraints, Mom had an inclination for ignoring personal boundaries. She would typically stake out her turf in the kitchen, the only room with a phone. Intimate calls, such as with my girlfriend, were a three-way conversation. I felt continually invaded. That made a day at the beach look good. But, as usual, my illusions were quickly shattered.

Our plan was to camp out at Uncle Al's property adjacent to Jones beach (the barrier reef protecting most of the south shore of Long Island) for a barbecue and some baseball, as we had done many times before. Inevitably the men and older boys ripped open cans of Bud and bottles of Ripple, getting as drunk as they could in the shortest amount of time.

"Okay, you motherfucker," my uncle would say, challenging Billie (his son and the oldest among us), "who's gonna be the first pussy here?"

More of the same followed from all sides, culminating with several of the men walking around with empty beer cans in their t-shirts to mimic breasts. That was the class act; it often deteriorated from there.

The alienation was intense. I longed for someone in the crowd of relatives, family, and friends to step forward, place a gentle hand around me, and say, "Have you read Vonnegut?" Or, "Tell me about your music and what amazes you." The disjuncture between who I was, and what my clan offered, felt painfully sharp.

Sitting around the dinner table was another rough-and-tumble experience. For starters, there was often not enough food. Mother was good at providing "fillers" like pasta and salad, but when it came to the "beef," portions were skimpy at best. Conversation

Even an intermittent brush with Bach or Beethoven helped to address my need to lift above the banal and enter the pearly gates of something I little understood, but felt a strong attraction to nevertheless.

was equally lean. In all my years at that table, not once did we talk about artists, writers, or musicians, and seldom the wider world.

So, early on, starting at around age eight, I began to unknowingly develop an inner life, one that would provide the contrasting richness and depth to my often disturbing home life. Making music was one important vehicle. Spending long hours in the practice room was not just about developing proficiency—more importantly, within those four walls, I was able to nurture the spaciousness that time alone in solitude could provide.

There was a timeless quality to making music that helped me transcend the ordinary for an occasional foray into the extraordinary. While my classical exposure was still minimal in childhood, even an intermittent brush with Bach or Beethoven helped to address my need to lift above the banal and enter the pearly gates of something I little understood, but felt a strong attraction to nevertheless.

Nature was another helpful refuge. I loved to take long, meandering walks in the woods. It was there, embraced by the complex and calming energy of the natural world, that I found shelter. The forest felt like home. It connected me to a living presence within that I felt very deeply, and that ameliorated the loneliness created by too superficial and combative an outer life.

I followed the paths of music and nature often as they led me gradually to locate a sense of inner peace, along with greater self-confidence and integration. By consistently revisiting that place inside, I began to believe in the rightness of it all. My trust that life is okay just the way it is began to take hold. Though I had no language for this at the time, my life as a seeker—a soul on a journey—had begun. I watched it emerge in the cramped quarters of my home and then move slowly, but surely, out into the wider world.

> *Though I had no language for this at the time, my life as a seeker—a soul on a journey—had begun.*

My middle years, roughly between the ages of thirty and sixty, mirrored childhood. On the surface I was a pretty typical high-achiever who enjoyed the accompanying material rewards while yearning for more. After a slow career start in my twenties, I finally found my stride in the next decade, discovering higher education as a supportive place to work, first as faculty, and then as an executive in colleges and universities.

It was in these relatively refined work environments that I discovered my innate talents and watched them flourish. But my rapid ascent from the street to the academy did not allow sufficient time for the strengthening of my inner self. Leftover insecurities from childhood were still plentiful. Deep inside I often felt like an imposter, asking myself what I was doing in this intellectually and culturally rich environment, having come from such an aggressive, raw family. When would I be found out?

I loved to swim at noon whenever my demanding schedule would permit. The college at which I was the Chief Financial Officer had a beautiful red-brick and steel athletic facility whose planning, design, financing, and construction I had overseen. On one typical day I ripped off my clothes, jumped into the pool, and banged out my customary two-thirds of a mile. Then I was off to shower, followed by a sprint back to the office.

As I began to dress, standing stark naked and feeling a bit vulnerable, Flint (one of the College room painters) walked up to me and said, "So, Mr. Merck, you come here at noon to look at all the sexy women in the pool, don't you?" He moved toward me in his grey baggy uniform, saying, "Come on, admit it. You're not any better than the rest. Us guys all love to look, don't we?"

I was mortified by his comments and frankly didn't know how to respond. The truth was that I hadn't even noticed the women in the pool. Not that I was above that kind of thing, I was just driven day after day to hop in, swim my laps, and get back to work for an afternoon of predictably challenging meetings. Of equal importance was the implicit institutional message: guys in my position didn't think those kinds of thoughts. And if we did, we certainly wouldn't talk about it openly.

This was not only a scrubbed-down Ivy League campus, it was a hotbed of early feminism—a place where the penalty for even tangentially sexist comments was to be hanged in the courtyard, and not by your neck. Plus, there was a double standard. The administrators—those of us that would regularly interface with the public—had to be fervently gender neutral. The college painters, and other similar employees hidden away in the bowels of the infrastructure could sit around the shop looking at scantily clad women while calling it just as they saw it.

Standing there physically naked, and now feeling psychically exposed, I wondered who it was that just swam those laps. Was it the average kid from Massapequa, Long Island, the one that had grown up in a neighborhood where cultural offerings consisted of *Reader's Digest* at best? Or was it the administrative officer and faculty member of a prestigious college? Could I reconcile these extremes? As with childhood, I was pushed inward to solidify my identity, to find a sustaining and nurturing energy that offered more than I could find in my choice of work environments.

Within a short timeframe I was entrusted with high levels of management responsibility, and compensated accordingly. Married and later blessed with a child, the picture became more or less complete. Here was your basic hardworking middle-aged guy who did well by making the most of his talents and living up to his responsibilities. There were also plenty of appealing opportunities on and off the job, which made for a fun-filled, experience-rich life.

I shared most of these with my wife Catherine. We moved together well, usually able to confront the joys and sorrows of life as if we were one. Without her support and love, my experience of the middle years would have been far less rewarding. Together we parented Evan and reaped the bounty of moving up the ladder financially and socially.

Oh, how I wish that were the end of the story. But it isn't. Similar to my childhood experience, there was always another tape running, a voice deep within that questioned the application of all that life energy. Wasn't there more than just the obvious—making money and taking on ever-increasing levels of responsibility? For more than thirty years I seemed to be stuck in the middle of an existential crisis, doing well and having fun, but longing for something more.

My spiritual yearning was further intensified by a gnarly psychological issue. Love—sweet nurturing love for just being alive—was in short supply in my childhood. Mother wasn't innately good at supplying it, plus she was distracted with four kids to worry about and inadequate financial resources to help keep the household afloat. Dad defined his role rather narrowly (like most men in the fifties and sixties) as the breadwinner and fix-it guy around the house, but not as the purveyor of unconditional love for his children. At least that was my reality.

For more than thirty years I seemed to be stuck in the middle of an existential crisis, doing well and having fun, but longing for something more.

But there *was* an area of parenting where both Mom and Dad generously dished out the accolades. It wasn't quite love, and it certainly wasn't unconditional, but at least we were given attention for anything that smacked of achievement, and the more socially visible the better. Whether with grades at school, merit badges at Boy Scouts, or performances at music recitals, the message was clear: achieve and ye shall be acknowledged.

I took this swap of attention for love with me into adulthood, now becoming the parent in abstention. Predictably, I was no more generous to myself than Mom and Dad had been. And, like in childhood, I received ever-higher levels of recognition in the form of loftier titles and increased compensation. But that became part of the problem. An achievement addiction is perhaps harder to shake than a substance addiction, since the societal response is mostly reinforcing.

Then, one day, as I was leaving to catch a flight, pain struck, and struck hard. It was so persistent that I remember uncharacteristically crying in front of Evan, at that time ten-years old, while screaming to god knows who for relief. It felt like someone was repeatedly stabbing my foot with an ice pick while squeezing my lower back muscles in a vice. Even though we were at home, Catherine called the college police, and within a few minutes a crew of my closest staff arrived to minister to their leader. I was deeply touched, which helped make the intense pain and deep anxiety it triggered a bit more tolerable.

When my back went into spasm, I was about ready to leave for a week of consulting, a side business I sustained alongside my full-time job as a college officer. In addition, I was also keeping up an aggressive performance schedule with the music department's premier ensemble. Basically three jobs, plus I took very seriously my role as both parent and spouse. Much of this I loved, of course, but the excessive nature of it, driven by my need to strive and achieve, was largely a frantic attempt at feeling loved.

The doctors said there was no evidence of physical abnormality, which confirmed what I intuitively knew. There was nothing *physically* wrong with me. Yes, there was major physical pain, but it wasn't being created by a physical abnormality. This was a scream—a very loud one—from my subconscious, telling me to back off and slow down. Now.

The back spasms had started in my late thirties. This was just the culmination at age fifty, and it wasn't a one-day ordeal. I was out of work with blinding hurt for two months, unable to walk, and occasionally suicidal. The feedback this time was strong enough to provide exactly what I needed: an unambiguous message to back off the achievement treadmill and start paying serious attention to loving myself unconditionally, while nurturing the more spiritual side of my being that had been crowded out in the interest of worldly success. In hindsight, this was my wake-up call. The pain was the bell—a very loud one—but I had been creating the path for years.

Day after day I sat in agony and prayed for insight. Drugs were useless. Catherine's love helped. It became increasingly obvious that nothing short of a major lifestyle change would moderate the anguish.

Then, one day, while hobbling to the bathroom from the chair I lived in, and slept in as well, I paused at the sink mirror to gaze inward. I mean really inward—deep through my eyes and into the soul behind. I held this posture for what seemed like an eternity. Magically, the pain stopped. As quickly as it had arrived, it was gone, but only when I made deep and sustained contact with the frightened soul within. As soon as I broke the connection, the intense discomfort would return.

I have revisited that place many times over the years. More than any healing gesture, it taught me the value of staying connected to my true self. It also instructed me how to love myself, and about my place in the world. And it taught me that physical pain can just as easily come from emotional or spiritual imbalance as it can from a physical abnormality.

Once the extreme throbbing abated, I brought back the keys to childhood balance, like making music and taking frequent walks in the forest. I also tried on a few new ones: yoga, meditation, reading spiritual self-help books, and other new-age activities. I had practiced yoga when I was in my twenties. This time though, I expanded my involvement, even to the point of becoming a teacher with upwards of three classes per week. It worked. Well, at least temporarily.

It taught me that physical pain can just as easily come from emotional or spiritual imbalance, as it can from a physical abnormality.

In short order I was back to feeling stronger and more balanced, but I was also surprised with an unintended consequence:

leaving my career. What had given me renewed strength to cope, also gave me the increased strength to leave it all behind. And so I did, at the youthful age of fifty-three, or 1999 on the calendar.

And I thought the back spasms were bad. It turned out that quitting work while pursuing a life without structure and a ready identity was a lot scarier than back pain. That's when the gears—my inner reality—began to grind in earnest. I had spent the better part of my adult life as a strategic planner and now the plan was to have… well, no plan. I needed to transition as quickly as I could from a professional who lived in the future to a guy who blissed out with ever-frequent, and ever-deeper forays into the moment. And all this laced with round-the-clock efforts to forgive and appreciate myself.

I had spent the better part of my adult life as a strategic planner and now the plan was to have...well, no plan. I needed to transition as quickly as I could from a professional who lived in the future to a guy who blissed out with ever-frequent, and ever-deeper forays into the moment.

Looking back, the folly of my assumption now seems quite humorous. Did I really think I would be able to switch gears and effortlessly move into a totally new way of life overnight, one that would embrace open-ended ambiguity? I had been paid well over the years to know, to be the manager who had all the answers. In contrast, I was being called to live more deeply from the space of not-knowing, the place Buddhists call "don't know mind."

So, in mid 2001, after spending an anxious year and a half lost in doubt and uncertainty, I made the obvious move and went back to work—nothing like a little distraction to keep the emotional goblins at bay. This time, though, I made some improvements in the nature of the work by starting my own consulting business, which afforded me greater freedom to continue with the retooling of Ed. I knew that retirement from full-time work would eventually come, but in that moment I just wanted a little diversion to help ease the pain of an overly steep learning curve.

Here I am back in 2009, and what an unpredictably wild ride it's been. I now understand that all this inner work, which began at age eight and continued to the present unabated, has been the training ground for my current transition into life's remaining chapters. My struggles with the shadows of a shaky childhood, and an outwardly fashioned middle life, served primarily to expand my interior capacity to cope with major change. And for that I am grateful, despite the often bumpy nature of the road.

> *I now understand that all this inner work... has been the training ground for my current transition into life's remaining chapters.*

This current transition may be the tsunami of personal transformation, but I feel equipped to meet it, having built my faith since childhood. Now it's time for a test drive.

For Edwin

(Dad)

You saw me when I didn't think you did

tuned to a deeper frequency all along.

Hearing my call of desperation

you responded by shining a light on my gift.

Music, yes, sweet music

the outpouring of your fatherly love,

and my ticket away from your earthly reality.

For Sabina

(Mom)

Why has it taken me so long to remember that you
love me?
To open again as in early childhood
to the sweetness between us
and the touching of our souls.
Listen, as we allow our vulnerabilities to merge
reestablishing that essential connection
between mother and son.
Sad, yes, that it has taken so long.
But glorious, indeed, that we have been reunited at last.

The Adult Sailor

5

On the Road...to Where?

Travelling west this first day on the road, I've come as far as Scranton. My ultimate destination is Southern Florida, where I'm to pick up my recently purchased boat—then sail north along the East Coast in time for summer back in the familiar waters of Southern New England.

I have no expectations about timing for the roughly 1,800 mile car trip—where I will stop and for how long—except for tonight. The plan is to meet a new and up-to-this-point virtual friend named Nancy somewhere close to Harrisburg. The allure of online dating, something I've dabbled in for years, has extended even into my trip. I'm eager to see if there is enough spark beyond the electronic flirtation to derail me from my trip to Florida. One can only hope for a traveler's miracle.

Several days prior to departure, I did a quick Google search for B&Bs near Harrisburg and found a few that looked interesting in a town named Paradise, of all things. *Well, I could use a little of that,* I thought. *How bad could a place named Paradise be?* As if to confirm my instincts, I noticed that the town immediately east of Paradise is named Intercourse.

Either I'm on to something big, or this is all just a cosmic setup. With my curiosity piqued, and my fingers crossed, I booked a room right at the Paradise/Intercourse border.

This last stretch of the drive today is along Route 30, which is proving to be a most unappetizing experience. To the left, right, and as far ahead as I can see, there is nothing but shopping outlets and strip malls. The natural beauty of the land has long ago been bulldozed away, leaving an ugly palette of cracked concrete, streaked macadam, and glaring neon lights. As I drive, traffic piles up frequently, making escape or detours difficult. *Do people really choose to live here*, I wonder? *Why do we inflict this on ourselves?*

Pulling up to the B&B late in the afternoon, I suddenly realize that the unappealing commercialism has stopped abruptly. In its place are luscious farms and open fields stretching far into the distance, and not the modern day agri-business farms, either. This is Amish Country that I have innocently stumbled into, with the B&B's location unexpectedly setting a clear boundary between what I have just struggled through, and a truly alluring sight up ahead.

Energized by the unexpected find, I change my clothes and go for a long walk through lush countryside. There before me are beautiful grains in various shades of soft yellow, interrupted occasionally by wood silos, tidy farm houses painted red, and large handmade barns for livestock. The farmers who till the fields are truly elegant at their work. They stand, lean in their simple garb, just forward of a combine that is pulled by a team of well-manicured and seemingly motivated draft horses. *Swish, swish* is all I can hear at a distance, and their continuous flowing movements are all I can see as the combine threshes the grain that will feed the cattle that will fertilize the land that will start the cycle all over again. It is mesmerizing. I first sit, and then eventually recline into a field of warm hay, absorbed by the teeming life all around me.

I can't help but wonder what lies beneath this simple life. At least through my eyes, there is an apparent sense of continuity and purpose. Here is a community whose very posture appears dignified, one that confidently announces, "We know who we are and what we are here to do." They seem totally engaged—not an observer among them. However physically taxing their lives, they are not sitting out this dance.

I know from previous reading that the Amish are Christocentric. Their unity as a sect comes from a strict adherence to scripture that proclaims a relative separation from worldly things, and a common and strongly adhered-to interpretation of their faith. At the risk of superimposing my own belief system onto theirs, I imagine that the communal unity they so strongly project comes also from their connection to the earth. I see them as having achieved a deep contentment that flows from their immersion in the land's natural rhythms. They can get to the end of the day and feel like there is a purpose to it all—that doing their work in such an honest and spiritual manner, *is the work*.

While lying in the field, looking through the strands of grain at the vast sky above, I'm reminded of my friend Mike from Foster. I am missing him, and the life I left behind. *This breaking away isn't going to be easy, despite what I am moving towards,* I overhear myself say.

More than anyone I have ever experienced, my buddy Mike best typifies someone who fully engages life. There isn't an observer bone in his body. We often find ourselves at opposite ends of the ideological spectrum, yet the love between us is deep and unquestionable. I'll never forget one of our first meetings way back in 2004, while strolling together through his vast gardens.

"Hey Michael" (I love to use the more formal version of his name as a way of signaling his dignity). "What the hell is this old style tub with bear claw feet doing in your garden, right here between the zucchini and the tomatoes?"

He smiled like I was just too pathetically naïve to understand. "For taking baths, what else, you dummy," he exclaimed. "Every morning I fill it up with cold well water. Most days, by evening the sun has warmed the water to a perfect temperature. Then I rip off my clothes and jump in. If there are any women in close proximity, all the better—and especially the curvy ones. You know what I mean, even if you do spend too much time behind that computer of yours."

Well, I did know what he meant, but I was also aware that I felt it—life force, that is—less than he did. He had a point about my sedentary lifestyle. Standing there feeling exposed in my overly tailored clothes, I sensed into my desire to be more like him.

Mike is a Zorba the Greek lookalike. He provides all his meat directly, and most of his vegetables. An avid hunter and fisherman, Mike raises his own chickens, and every year a pig and one beef cow. His vegetable gardens are the envy of many, and his work includes splitting wood by hand (about 140 cords a year). No TV, never any prepared food, and the best cooking I've had anywhere. From seed to meal, he embraces it all. Plus, he tells a lot

Now I want to feel fully alive; to see in my eyes the same light I witness in Mike's, and the same physical flow I observe in the Amish at work.

of good jokes—a sign, I have always thought, of his love for life and his belief in the implicit humor (or is it catastrophe?) of the human condition. Oh, and at *seventy,* he can out arm-wrestle any man or woman for miles around. His blindingly intense, and light-filled blue eyes brim over with a vitality that makes him appear as vibrant as any thirty-year-old I have ever known.

The spirit of both Mike and the Amish remind me of a primary reason I committed to this journey: to live out-of-doors in a manner that continuously engages the environment. After decades of work that kept me inside—mostly behind a desk—this transition is in part about reclaiming my connection to the outside world. I need my body, mind, and spirit to reengage directly with the earth and sea—to feel that raw energy coursing through my veins. While my work in management and strategic planning has been financially good to me over the years, it hasn't been about moment-to-moment contact with the elements. Now I want to feel fully alive; to see in my eyes the same light I witness in Mike's, and the same physical flow I observe in the Amish at work.

It will be mid-afternoon before I can pull away from this thought-provoking place. But first-up on that crisp morning in late May is my planned meeting with Nancy. Even though I am filled with fresh insights, things do not bode well. I can feel it in my bones.

I watch who I think is Nancy drive up to Eddie's Diner, our appointed rendezvous. Grey Camry, blue shirt, freshly washed brown hair. She waits to get out of her car, perhaps summoning courage. Once inside, simply in the way she smiles and hesitates over ordering, the uncertain things she does with her hands, and her generally angular movements, I feel no chemistry between us. She is attractive enough, and can carry an interesting conversation about important topics, but I have no interest in lingering, no desire to know the spaces she inhabits.

I learned many years ago to trust my instincts, and this is no time for a departure. Funny—I've run my life pretending to follow a path based primarily on rational evidence. (That's what you would expect from a Chief Financial Officer, isn't it?) But the truth is that I felt my way all along. Most critical decisions—whether they were in management, finance, or most importantly, in the realm of women—always flowed from intuition.

Regardless of my instincts, and perhaps hers, Nancy and I still have to entertain each other for at least a few hours, no matter what. These are the unwritten rules. Why didn't I see this coming? If my intuition is so well-honed, why didn't I figure this out ahead of time and avoid the discomfort?

In my experience, the electronic medium offers an initial link that can easily be misleading. It is just damn hard to read someone when you can't feel their vibes. And while online dating provides a wide pool of candidates, these options are often deceptive. If I'd met Nancy at a friend's party, we would have known the bad news in a flash and found a quick excuse to move on. But here amid the ketchup and fries, we go through a polite and tedious dance to unwind what we created electronically. Driving away, I muse that she is a prank from the universe, playing on my capacity to fantasize, and fueled by the provocative names of Paradise and Intercourse. As usual, I have much yet to learn, and especially when it comes to the opposite gender.

Back on the road, I smile, realizing that I'm not going to make Florida in the customary two days my family has always spoken of. Thankfully, I've moved far enough away from my achievement compulsion for it not to matter. I fight my way back west to Route 81, encountering traffic volume only a pleasant Saturday of Memorial Day weekend could produce. Finally, I'm once again heading south.

This is only day two of the trip, a little more than twenty-four hours since leaving my house, but it feels like several years. Settling into the drive, I'm reminded of a handwritten note that pointed to the perceptual tricks time can play on us. I discovered it in my packing phase just a few weeks ago when it dropped out of nowhere and announced itself as important. On a small two-inch square piece of dark brown parchment, the following words were written in red ink:

> *Days are long*
> *Years are short*
> *Surrender*

I kept shuffling the piece of paper aside as it followed me around the house like an insistent packing partner. I even tried to destroy it, but finally gave in and realized that maybe there was a message here for me.

Is this advice something obvious, like being grateful for each experience so as to get the most out of the short time we have? Or is it something deeper—perhaps an invitation from the universe to slow down and allow my heart to open more fully? Or maybe something existential, like a reminder that time—life, really—is infinitely expandable and collapsible.

And what about that last word, surrender? I know from practicing meditation that my sense of time changes as I let go deeper into the moment. Quite naturally, my mind softens its grip on the past and the future as I fall into that delightful space of "now." Even my heart becomes more receptive as the pace of my mind slowly modulates from fast to...well, not so fast.

Is surrendering really the key to happiness, and is that the implied secret in the note? Is it as simple—and as difficult—as letting go?

Back to the road. The terrain quickly becomes interesting. South from Harrisburg takes me almost immediately into the foothills of the Appalachian Mountains. Then follows the big stuff: the majestic peaks and valleys of first West Virginia, then Virginia. It all happens rather rapidly, and by early evening I'm well into northern Virginia.

Unlike the day before, I haven't identified a resting place for the evening (no potential romance this time). Where to stop? The choices seem limitless, yet unanimously unappealing. Endless miles of characterless motels line the sides of the highway, each hoping to net as many weary travelers as possible.

Suddenly, there it is, high up on the hill. It looks like all the rest, yet it seems to call to me—or am I just too tired to hold out any longer? Pulling into the parking lot of a no-frills motel called The Wayfarer, I wonder about the integrity of my intuitions. Pushing ahead, though, I check in as quickly as possible, requesting a room facing away from the highway on the top floor at the very end—sheltered from as much noise and distraction as possible.

I park the car, retrieve my overnight bag, and climb the stairs to my room. Once in, the smell of formaldehyde from the carpeting is enough incentive for me to move quickly onto the balcony. Then, looking out, I immediately see the reason I've ended up here. Framed like a Monet, the bucolic scene before me is as vast as it is peaceful. Just beyond the parking lot, an emerald green field emerges. It is a 270-degree view, rising gently toward the horizon as if to defy gravity. The grass has been recently cut, and a sprinkle of rain helps to bring out the intensity of its color and scent. At the top of the hill is a weathered red barn which strikes a comforting contrast with the surrounding green grass. Completing the picture, dotted all along the hill sit lazy, relaxed, white cows with handsome, wide black bands around their middles.

After a long day in the car, this painterly scene draws me slowly back into my body, breath by breath. I can't bear to only glance at the lovely picture and go back into the room. Instead, propping open the door, I drag an easy chair to the opening, and gaze out. Resting aimlessly, a sense of wellness descends, as if I am a part of the peaceful landscape. In

Is surrendering really the key to happiness? Is it as simple—and as difficult—as letting go?

contrast, turning back to the room with its stark utilitarian furnishings, a palpable sense of aloneness pervades. Such natural beauty reconnects me to myself. I am totally absorbed in the landscape, and feel like time has stopped.

Sitting there, I remember a scene from *Doctor Zhivago* where Uri, who is stuck in a cattle car under some of the most squalid and dehumanizing of conditions, slides open a small wooden window to view the stunning snow-capped Urals in the distance. For that moment he is transported from the foul to the majestic. *We do create our own reality,* I think. *Even beauty is totally subjective.*

Contemplating sleep, I move inside and try opening the single window. Locked, of course. Besides doing everything they can to neuter the room, the designers secured the windows so that temporary occupants can't expose ourselves, or the room, to the variable elements. Isn't "No Surprises," the signature phrase of The Holiday Inn chain? Since when did being surprised become a problem?

There is no way I'm going to bolt myself in this room, breathe artificial air all night, and sever the connection with the natural world I've been cultivating for the past few hours. A simple solution emerges: shut off the air conditioner, prop open the door, lie down on the bed with a view towards the meadow, feel the peace, and fall asleep. I figure no one will mess with me overnight since, from the looks of it, I am definitely certifiable. Besides, the other occupants are all locked in their rooms.

> *We do create our own reality... Even beauty is totally subjective.*

In the morning I quickly shower, organize, and head down to the office, where a continental breakfast has been advertised. Taking one look at the white bread, sugar-coated cereal, and the back-country version of hot cross buns, I bow and leave. But I'm happy as a clam in mud or, more locally, a grass-fed black and white cow grazing in a gorgeous meadow. Driving out of the parking lot, I think, *This is the best thirty-nine dollars I've ever spent.*

I don't stop for breakfast, choosing instead to fill up on two of my favorite traveling foods, which are already handy in the car: carrots and peanut butter. I know, it doesn't sound as appetizing as bacon, eggs, and buttered rye toast, but trust me, it is nutritious, filling, and tastes good. If the peanut butter jar is more than half full, you can dunk your carrot in, scrape up a little PB, and you're good. If the jar is less than half full, you can use a knife or—even better—heat it up a bit (that's what car heaters are for), and dribble it on. If no one is looking, break open that jar of homemade strawberry jam and double dunk. Yum. After you're hooked, permission granted to pass the idea on to your friends.

Early morning, and the odometer reads only a little over 650 miles—not much to show for two days. What will brother Tom say when I make my trip report? Here I am at the beginning of day three and I'm not even halfway. Further complicating things, I'm beginning to think that there's no actual destination: that *there* doesn't even exist.

Why rush anyway? Wouldn't I risk short-circuiting an important exercise in self-exploration, only to put a few additional miles under my feet? Don't we go on trips to open up space for reflection, to sidestep all the mundane responsibilities and all the to-do lists, for the spaciousness of the road? Don't we travel to allow what needs attention at the moment to come forward and to revel— without judgment if we are lucky—in the surprising forces that lie waiting beneath the surface? Are our efforts to attribute meaning beyond that but veiled attempts to sustain the illusion of control, and the fantasy of our own importance?

During most of my work years I had a favorite postcard tacked to the office door. It was a graphic of the Milky Way, filled with silvery dots and an arrow pointing to one of them with the caption "You Are Here." If that message wasn't sobering enough, the flip side carried more punch: "Our planet Earth is one of several billion stars in the Milky Way, which is one of several billion galaxies in the Universe." For me, it was a poignant reminder that we are far less important than we think. And for those entering the office, I hoped the message would be: let's just relax a bit and make the most of this moment, this connection between us. Isn't that all we really have? As a dear friend of mine is fond of saying, "The being here now *is* the outcome."

My trip is through some of the most spectacular scenery in the Eastern United States. I intentionally chose to head south via the "inside" route rather than hug the coastline, and today is the biggest payoff. The coastal route, which sounds much better than it is, principally takes you through one intense population center after another and all the accompanying joys: traffic, eighteen-wheelers, smog, heat, and humidity. By avoiding the big-city coastal corridor, I'm being treated to the impressive backcountry before reconnecting with the coastal route in Georgia for the final stretch south.

Route 81 and then Route 77 through Virginia, North Carolina, and South Carolina embrace some of the great scenic passageways in America. Haltingly breathtaking, they parallel the Appalachian Mountain chain and run through rugged, richly forested land for the better part of four-hundred miles. Unlike the Blue Ridge Mountain Highway, the Interstate does not ride the crest of the mountains, but I still feel as if I've been surfing the waves and feeling the thrill of the lift, just like the take-off moment in sailing or flying.

The day is speeding by as I sense full immersion in every moment. I'm already at the outskirts of Savannah, having traveled six-hundred miles in what feels like less than an hour. Is this another perceptual shift, like that suggested by the short poem I left behind? Can days change from tedious to short and sweet, just by being more present? I've

"The being here now is the outcome."

surrendered to the road and its long string of moments; now the odometer shows more miles than if I'd *tried* to make this a chest-thumping day.

As Savannah grows near, I realize that making a choice for the evening stopover is close at hand. There is no way I'm going to top the $39 special, that beautiful expansive field, or the grazing cows. So I listen to my inner guidance system, which says to skip over Savannah, despite its proximity and abundance of interesting sites. Exploration of its heralded beauty and related southern charm will have to wait for another day.

Holding my breath, I take the next exit and begin hunting around. Almost immediately there appears before me a brand-new motel, whose back end faces directly into a lovely wooded area. It has a room that looks onto the forested spot all right, but in contrast to the night before, the space itself turns out to be richly appointed with marble, leather, and the like. Completely over the top, it also has a much appreciated comfy bed. While not $39, at less than $100 it still seems like a good deal.

The place is a little spooky though. During the entire time I'm here, I see or hear no one, even when leaving in the morning. It mystifies me why I appear to be the only customer, especially since the Holiday Inn next door, which looks out on nothing but ugly parking lots, is brimming over with customers. Nonetheless, I sleep peacefully, connected to the energy of the forest while sinking luxuriously into the down-filled bed. Sometimes it's better not to question the blessings that come our way, or who is sending them.

Upon waking, I realize that this is it: day four. I have only three hundred miles to go before Cocoa Beach, Florida, my temporary stopping point for a few days. Then I will head further south to Fort Lauderdale, where repairs to

Sometimes it's better not to question the blessings that come our way, or who is sending them.

my boat are being completed. Cocoa Beach is on Florida's East Coast, just below Cape Canaveral, home of NASA and most space-related activity of the last forty years. It is the town where my parents bought a condo fronting the Banana River looking west, with the Atlantic Ocean a short walk to the east. They enjoyed winter in the Sunshine State sandwiched between these two impressive bodies of water.

I nurtured a cozy connection over the last year to this small, sweet, quiet place that rests less than fifty feet from the river, and within a half mile of the ocean. Most notable during these visits was my sense of being surrounded by water. Reach out and it was there, go to sleep and I felt immersed in it, swim in it and I became it. There was no mistaking the palpable feel of aqua energy (some claim archetypically feminine energy) all around me, all of the time. And the quieter I got, the more dominant it became.

While driving along, fond memories of connecting again to this condo by the river make today's four-hour ride feel like a slow-motion slide into home base. The image in my mind is one of coasting down a gentle slope, like a very long water slide at a theme park, including a splash at the end.

This is exactly what happens. I drive straight through to Cocoa Beach, change into my bathing suit, and promptly dive into the Atlantic. It feels like an important part of my journey has both come to a close and opened up, all at the same moment.

Waiting at the Dock

6
Getting Free

In my mind, this Cocoa Beach stopover is going to be just that—a brief pause in an otherwise linear series of events that connects the dots from land to sea, from house to sailboat. No real significance, just a place to catch my breath for a few days while repairs to the boat are completed.

I estimate the work will take two days, so I don't even unpack the car at first, believing with certainty that this is a limited engagement. Of course, thinking we know anything with certainty, especially about how our lives will unfold over time, is one of the great mind-traps of life. As usual, I fall right into it.

The dreaded phone calls start almost immediately. Antonio, the seasoned head of the boatyard, tries to deliver the news in a measured way.

"Sorry, Eduardo, but the repairs—especially those that need days of clear, dry weather—are going to be much more extensive than we first thought." I hear him inhale as though he's told a dozen customers the same thing without a positive response. "As you can see by looking out the window, the weather is all about rain. And it's predicted to stay that way for awhile." He pauses. I hear clanging in the background and the roar of an acetylene torch. "The parts we ordered are delayed, and the boat handlers only work on weekdays. Plus, they are really in need of a vacation right about now. Are you getting the picture?"

No, I am not getting the picture, I think to myself. *At least not in a productive way.* Instead of seeing this as an opportunity to enjoy Cocoa Beach for as long as it takes to finish the work, my inner executive flares up big time. I am determined to move this along at a speed that will get me sailing in a few short days.

I watch myself go from being a tolerant customer to losing it. "Antonio, what the hell? I thought my boat would be finished by now, back in the water, and ready to go. That was the plan and you agreed to it. I'm tired of all your excuses. Just put whatever resources you need on this project and make it happen, yesterday."

Of course, thinking we know anything with certainty, especially about how our lives will unfold over time, is one of the great mind-traps of life.

"Look, man," he says, with obvious irritation in his voice, "I can't apply fiberglass in the rain, and that's all it's been doing for over a month now. There's been some rain every day, and sometimes a virtual flood." I can tell he's struggling to keep his composure. "I need at least three consecutive dry days. When that happens, you'll have your boat back. Until then, just chill out, and try not to call me so often."

Chill out. What the hell is he talking about? I want my boat, and I want it *now*. For years I've been living out of a core belief that life events take on the shape *I* give them. In my mind, the road to happiness is simply about deciding what I want, making a plan to get there, and putting the requisite energy into making it happen. So where is my finished boat? Why am I not already on the water?

My irritation increases with each passing day, yet the harder I push, the longer my boat is delayed. Why isn't life unfolding as I envisioned? Is this merely a problem of expectations?

Forget, and I did, about the pleasure of a swim in the ocean, abundant yoga classes, a health food co-op to satisfy any vegetarian's desires, breathtaking views of the Banana River, a rich spiritual community to tap into, accessible restaurants of every imaginable type and ethnicity, and a peaceful, quiet location.

Why isn't life unfolding as I envisioned? Is this merely a problem of expectations?

Not to mention, but I will, that it's rent free. No, I have convinced myself that fulfillment and joy are somewhere else, a place closer to my design and expectations, but not here in Cocoa Beach, and certainly not right now. I can almost hear the universe laughing, having found in me such a gullible student to work with.

Partly out of desperation—always one of my best teachers—I begin searching for a different way, one that is less painful. Even I can back my ego down a few notches if the pain is strong enough. Maybe I need to more fully open to what is already familiar—the Buddhist wisdom inherent in the yogic path. After all, I have been both practicing and teaching that path for almost a decade now. Isn't it time for me to walk the talk?

So, instead of willfully trying to create life according to my design, I begin experimenting with different yogic mind postures designed to loosen the grip of my expectations. Slowly and quite naturally, the contrasting (and more positive) energy of acceptance begins to flow. As I grow closer to accepting what is, to simply embracing the reality before me, life takes on a quality that is decidedly more satisfying.

It feels like the sky is opening up, and I'm beginning to see patches of blue again. I begin to walk the beach every day. Sometimes twice a day. And not just short, leisurely strolls. These are serious five-to-six mile walks, giving me the time to immerse myself in the beauty and rhythms of this natural wonderland.

The beach at Cocoa is truly wonderful—as good an example of expansive beauty as I've seen anywhere. Reassuringly repetitive, its palette offers miles and miles of breathtaking white sand, punctuated only intermittently with sea grass and mangrove trees. The sand is hard-packed, which allows for extended multiple-mile walks without stress to my legs and feet. And just in case boredom begins to loom, there are almost always numerous distractions of the scantily clad curvy variety frolicking in the surf.

"Antonio, how's it going?" I ask with surprising calm.

"I told you, Eduardo," he says in his distinct Spanish accent, "when Southern Florida gets a few dry days, we'll work. Until then—"

"OK, Antonio ," I cut him off. "I got it. Just let me know when the clouds pass." *Why did I even call him?* Old habits die hard.

I've come to love my walks on the beach—time alone, yet I'm also in the presence of walkers, dreamers, surf fishermen, and sunbathers. Individually and collectively, we all share in communion with the vastness of the ocean, feeling connected to it and to each other. This is the special place where land meets sea, a place of abundant creative energy. And it feels like each day yields a new unfolding of me. No more daily calls to Antonio—the boat will be ready when the boat is ready. Surrender to the inevitability of the universe may be a tough act, but right now it feels very gratifying. So on I walk, with a growing smile on my face.

Once I stop arguing with the way life is, I begin to discover many other delights. (Is this really cause and effect?) On the periphery of the condominium complex is a first-class food co-op. The Sunseed has been in existence since the late sixties, replete with a nutrition and supplement section which more than rivals the much talked about Whole Foods Market. Here, I find organic everything without even a hint of white flour, sugar, or preservatives. There is also a great selection of organic wines and beers, and lots of seasonal local produce. Plus, most of the help are volunteers committed to building a strong community, one dedicated to healthy connections with food and to each other.

"Hey bro, what's the best organic beer of the week?" I ask Jason, the co-op manager, whom I've come to know.

"Try this pint of Brother Thelonious," he suggests amiably, "Got a good head and the right amount of malt."

I knew the Monk from his jazz, and this brew turns out to be equally good in its own right. The "brother" had it right in so many ways. Even more than the beer, I grow to really love the daily connection with like-minded folk at the Sunseed, this hippie-style throwback to my youth. It is relaxed, honest, and with no detectable bullshit.

"Breathing in, breathing out. Breathing in, breathing out. Breathing in, I soften my body; breathing out, I feel peaceful. Breathing in, I calm my mind; breathing out, I feel joy." Every morning our faithful yoga teacher leads us through the same opening lines. And each day the rhythm of my breath draws me inward to a place of greater peace and acceptance. Roxanne isn't the most spiritual yoga teacher I've experienced, but she delivers a good, clean routine. Her focus is clearly on the physical plane, with a few spiritual moments thrown in to temper her touch. But that is fine with me. Sailing can be rigorous, and these routines will help prepare me for the physical challenges of life at sea.

Roxanne presents her class in a generously sized studio, contiguous to the Sunseed. It is part of an alternative health center that offers classes in yoga, Zen meditation, Chi Gong, and Tai Chi. Besides the classes, there is also a full menu of health care treats: acupuncture, gentle chiropractic, and body/energy work in multiple modalities, including several types of massage. I love the center and begin taking full advantage of its gifts.

Roxanne starts in with, "Breathing in, breathing out."

Suddenly, my mind screams *Hogwash. I'm supposed to be going deeper into the spiritual moment, and all I can focus on is Roxanne's shapely body.*

One day after the others have left, she says, "Maybe you'd like to teach a few classes for me." I smile at the thought. "I know you'd be softer and have a more spiritual approach," she adds. "Plus, I'd love to learn something from you." She offers all this with a warm, inviting, and—to my ears—seductive tone.

"Sure," I say. "That would be great," fighting back my animal instincts to show her a few highly unorthodox yoga postures right then and there.

I end up teaching a few of her classes, while calming myself down enough to do a decent job under the circumstances. We even have lunch a few times after class, where I find her green cotton shirt and coral tights more tempting then her yoga sweats. But Roxanne's implied self assessment is correct: she is Miss Yoga Light. Plus—and this is the real deal-breaker—she is fifteen years younger than me (part of the reason for my raw attraction, I'm sure). I know there is nothing sustainable in that.

... that the universe is constantly changing, and peace of mind comes out of listening and accepting, not planning and directing.

Better not to get in too deep, Ed, my subconscious offers. Plus, I am only in Cocoa until my boat is ready anyway—not a good time to start up something new and this hot. So, I cut off the subtle flirting, and we both go back to doing our downward-facing dogs like true yogis.

Frequenting the Cocoa Beach Library, a virtual town center devoted to building community, expands me. Elder folk read and recreate cheek-to-jowl with families, all interested in the cultural and intellectual offerings of this attractive, light-filled space. Books, lectures, and live music are regular fare. Plus, either on the way back to the condo or later the same evening, I often take pleasure in one of the many fine and mostly reasonably priced ethnic restaurants.

Initially during my stay in Cocoa, attempts at superimposing a static life-plan over a dynamic universe led only to frustration. Now I seem more ready to embrace the truth, as simple and as deceptively obvious as it is; that the universe is constantly chang-

... release from suffering and willfulness will come only after I more fully let go of expectations, and my perceived need to control outcomes.

ing, and peace of mind comes out of listening and accepting, not planning and directing.

Have I come full circle? Has the so-called stopover in Cocoa turned into a full-blown connection to place? And has the silent hand behind it all used this time to prepare me for life ahead, despite my resistance?

As I embrace these questions, my belly gently softens. Then, almost simultaneously, the phone rings with Antonio's voice on the line. "Eduardo, your boat will be ready in a few days—this time for sure."

Ah, a result I tried to force, and failed at miserably, finally emerges *after* I stop trying to make it happen. My hard-earned lesson is clear: release from suffering and willfulness will come only after I more fully let go of expectations, and my perceived need to control outcomes.

Am I getting closer to a more comfortable fit with this next life-stage? I ask myself. And on a more practical note, *Am I ready for the sail north and all the challenges it will bring?*

Kairos

7

Opportune Moment

Leaving Cocoa Beach is turning out to be more difficult than I thought. It has taken me the better part of six weeks to positively embrace the reality of an extended stay and now, just when I receive the go-ahead to move on, I'm feeling unsettled again.

What's happening here? I've gotten what I wanted, so why the discomfort? Why does an activity as seemingly innocuous as packing the car for my departure trigger apprehension? If I really left home to catch up with my spirit, as my deepest instincts inform me, why is this relatively minor release from familiarity so disquieting?

My stay in Cocoa, despite initial reluctance, eventually became enjoyable. I put down roots by meeting people I liked, getting to know my way around town, and doing the infinite number of tasks that help a

... my experience has been that change is ultimately where the juice is.

person—like the spider and his web—spin a sense of place. Now I am once again severing the ties that provide for a sense of belonging. Ugh.

Part of me wants life to stay put for a while. I want to believe, despite all evidence to the contrary, that permanence is possible, and that the vicissitudes of change can be dampened just by freezing the moment.

But I know better. Notwithstanding the occasional anxiety that comes from engaging the unknown, my experience has been that change is ultimately where the juice is. It's what has kept me alive and vibrant over the years. Sure, I've been plenty tempted to believe that safety and comfort lie in repetition. That all I have to do is find the sweet spots of life, build up a healthy catalogue, and repeat the tunes at will. Yet on the occasions when I gave in to that approach, my life always lost its freshness. It felt as if I were living a lie, one that had me believing in the myth that I could control my experiences in order to achieve predictable outcomes.

My heart longs for a more imaginative and interesting life. That's why I am going to the sea, to feel the vitality that comes from living life on the edge. I want to feel life's wildness in my veins as I embrace the vivacity of the unknown. I want to metaphorically jump out of that plane and enjoy the freefall without clinging to things, feelings, or even states of mind. I want to drop my attempts at holding on, trusting instead in the capacity and love of the universe. This is my destiny, and I can hear its call like the urge to be born again.

I want to metaphorically jump out of that plane and enjoy the freefall without clinging to things, feelings, or even states of mind.

Despite feelings of unsettledness, I finish packing the car and begin the drive south. The trip is going to take less than four hours, hardly enough time to settle into anything substantive. Along the way, I do flirt with the awkwardness of feeling in between, with no tangible roots to call home. *Better get used to it*, I think. There will be plenty of that coming up, since living on a sailboat quite literally means occupying a residence that is continually in motion.

Even at anchor, the view from any porthole constantly changes as wind shifts frequently reposition the craft. And while there is a predictably challenging aspect to this life of constant variation, there are also some obvious advantages, like keeping my visual field fresh and invigorating. Plus, this will be a great way, I figure, to damp down boredom and keep me present to the ever-changing nature of things.

I time my arrival in Fort Lauderdale to coincide with the scheduled launch. Entering through the gates of the boat yard, I see her up on the travel lift, ready to be lowered into the water after the yard workers return from their lunch break. My heart skips a few beats—she looks regal, all thirty-six feet of her (forty-two counting the bowsprit). The love is clearly still there as I gaze adoringly at her beamy white hull, rimmed with a beautiful blue stripe. Above deck she sports a full complement of white sails, including two head sails that define her as a stately cutter—not just a mere sloop. It has been almost three months since I last saw her, and absence has certainly made my heart grow fonder. Beautiful lines, a tight new fiberglass bottom, bright and shiny topsides—what more could a sailor ask for?

It was in the spring of 2008, about one year ago, that I began taking more seriously my strong and long-held desire to sail fulltime. In the months that followed, the idea became increasingly palpable. Amidst doubts and apprehensions, I started searching for boats online. The analogy to online dating didn't escape me as I investigated the boat yards and dealer listings for sloops and ketches, yawls and schooners, homemade boats and designer racers. The choices were tantalizing, but each had their flaws—too old, poorly maintained, too expensive, too fussy, too utilitarian, no pizazz.

And then, on vacation in January of 2009, I saw *Kairos*. She was in Florida, ten years old, and with lines that were this sailor's dream. Like all boats, she needed repairs. One of the renovations I had commissioned and now notice with pleasure is her refurbished name, proudly displayed on the stern. While admiring the facelift, I reflect upon my first inquiry to the broker about the "yacht for sale."

"Do you know anything about her name?" I asked.

He replied with an abrupt, "No," as if that was an odd and even irrelevant question.

But I thought differently, perhaps looking for a sign that this was the boat for me. Hanging up, I immediately went to Wikipedia for the definitive scoop, keeping my fingers crossed.

Bingo. Our modern online encyclopedia offered the literal definition of "opportune moment." That certainly grabbed my attention. Apparently the Greeks have two names for time: Kronos, which they think of as clock or human-structured time; and Kairos, which I'll sum up here as spiritual time, or time of the gods. So, Kronos—external reference point; Kairos—internal reference point. Kronos—artificially structuring the future, and Kairos—going deeper into the present moment.

I sat back in my chair and smiled, knowing that this was the affirmation I had been searching for. Here was a potential home for me whose very *name* represented the life I was moving toward, one that I hoped would eventually lead me to a richer and more vibrant inner life. There ensued several months of wrapping my head around the decision to buy *Kairos,* and several more in negotiating the practical details, but I knew intuitively at the time that this was the *opportune moment,* and that she would eventually be my "sailing girl."

Now back at the dock the work crew returns from lunch right on schedule and instantly lowers *Kairos.* As her waterline gently meets the sea, I excitedly jump aboard. The feel of her underfoot is wonderful. She is solid and beautifully made: the teak detailing on the deck, the polished fittings, the new lines and sheets, the signature brass dolphin ornament—all of her.

The smell of varnish, glues, newly applied fiberglass, and myriad finishes all blend into a kind of sexy sailor's cologne, furthering my intoxication.

"Whoa baby" I call aloud as I open the engine compartment to check out the new alternator belts and the rerouting of fuel lines. Turning to the men in the shop, I say, "Great job. Looks terrific. I could almost eat my morning eggs on top of the engine."

Rodriguez, the yard foreman, bellows back in his contrasting laid-back style, "Yeah, man, we enjoyed working on your boat. Not often we get something of her quality round here."

After checking the newly installed gas gauge, radar, and compass (and no longer able to contain myself), I crank up the engine and take off for a short ride down the river to my pre-arranged dock space. Over the next few days I attend to many last-minute mechanical adjustments while provisioning her with food, safety equipment, nautical charts, and other essential gear for the trip north.

But this is not going to be a solo gig, either during the final preparation phase or the trip itself. I need an expert captain and crew who can cope with whatever boat and nature choose to throw at us. Sailing on the open ocean, and preparing the vessel before departure, are not activities for the inexperienced. Without competent mechanics and a skilled delivery team the risk is great, and the potential consequences grave.

Naturally, my selection of crew is governed by my own limitations. I am a relatively inexperienced blue water or open-ocean sailor, despite having sailed the coast of New England for over thirty years, with occasional forays into Floridian and Caribbean waters. In many ways coastal sailing is more difficult, since it requires avoiding obstacles of all types. Shallow water, rocks, docks, sunken vessels, and of course other craft, are often just an oar's distance away in crowded harbors. Then there are dramatic tides, currents, and erratic wind patterns that can take you substantially off course.

Blue water sailing is mostly about setting a direction, affecting alterations in strategy as weather and sea conditions change, and finding the stamina to be on watch for other vessels—especially at night. There is of course much overlap between coastal and blue water sailing. The big difference is that when something goes wrong, and you are two-hundred miles from the nearest land mass, the fix is often more difficult, and the stakes a whole lot higher.

I'll need two crew members, since the magic number for a small-to-medium-sized sailboat on an extended passage is three. This provides enough room for two to sleep comfortably at any one time, yet gives enough shift coverage for each person to have at least six hours of shuteye every evening.

It's a given that one of the two remaining slots will be filled by Evan, now a tall, handsome, quick-witted, and highly capable guy's guy. (Women love him also.) At twenty, he is sharper than me, more adept at electronics, physically stronger, and far less intimidated under pressure (I tell myself he doesn't know enough yet to be scared). But while his youth adds necessary diversity of a type, his sailing portfolio is similar to mine: coastal and relatively mechanically inexperienced. That makes the choice of the third team member even more important.

Enter Brett, whom we anoint Captain Brett, with all the responsibility and authority attributed to that designation. At forty-two, Brett is shorter than average but wiry, quick-footed, and a bit of a contortionist. He can fit above, under, or around any mechanical system that needs his immediate or sustained attention. And he possesses an extensive blue water delivery resume, with all the Coast Guard approvals to back it up. More importantly, he is the most talented mechanical genius I have ever worked with other than my father—the king of fix-it guys—who still holds that distinction, even into my seventh decade.

Fortunately, Brett is available when I make the call, which solidifies a three-person crew for the journey north with youth

(Evan), maturity (me), and someone who really knows what the hell he's doing when it comes to both ocean sailing and boat maintenance (Brett).

Drawing up to the dock, my mind is suddenly, and surprisingly flooded with shocking thoughts. *Sure, Ed, you've prepared well, but… do you really have the underlying confidence to pull this off? At sixty-three, are you just too damn old? Did you wait too long? Are you putting your life—and Evan's—on the line?* Throwing off the dock lines to an innocent bystander, I vow to reengage this conversation later. Well, maybe. No time now for self-doubt.

Evan flies down from New York, and Brett drives up from Miami. We have our first meal together in the cockpit of *Kairos*, safely tied to the canal dock just one day after I pick her up at the boatyard. This is summer, and it sure is hot—upwards of 102 degrees during

At sixty-three, are you just too damn old?

the day. But despite the oppressive heat, the initial meeting flows well. We'll be spending a minimum of ten days together round the clock in a very small space with nowhere to go, and there are sure to be some very stressful times ahead that will require a coordinated approach to resolving conflict.

Our trip will be a serious one—roughly 1,400 nautical miles in a relatively small sailing vessel with a maximum average speed of six knots, a pace only equivalent to twice that of a brisk walk. Even if we were able to sail nonstop from our starting point of Fort Lauderdale, Florida, to our end point at Martha's Vineyard, Massachusetts, the trip would take 234 hours or approximately ten continuous days. Not exactly what I am used to with coastal sailing, where every night is spent in a protected harbor.

Sailors call this the "shakedown" cruise, an opportunity to ferret out any remaining and as yet unaddressed mechanical kinks. We have done everything possible in controlled circumstances to bring the boat up to cruising standards, but I know that when we test those efforts in real-time through intense weather conditions, the unapparent weaknesses hidden from us under low-stress conditions are sure to surface. And when they do, we aren't going to be sitting comfortably in a boatyard with plenty of mechanics just a shout away.

It is now a game of wait and see. What will the ocean throw at us, and how will we fare?

Evan and His Prize

8
Flirting with Impermanence

It is July in Florida, usually an unstable time for weather patterns, but this year has been particularly extreme.

During the prior weeks, I watched safely from the Cocoa Beach condo as the ominous moisture-filled clouds rolled from west to east. They struck a broad target with their impressive electrical show sporting winds strong enough to bend over even the most robust of palm trees. While witnessing this phenomenon, I anxiously reviewed the drill in my head as if on *Kairos*: drop the sails immediately, secure all loose lines or anything that could move on its own, and proceed cautiously under engine power.

Now, first night out on the water, the dreaded weather moves in, testing our cohesiveness as a crew. I've seen the storms coming for quite a while, since views at sea are unobstructed, especially from our current vantage point some fifty miles offshore. Huge dark clouds shoot out vertical jolts of bright light every few seconds, and for reasons beyond my amateur understanding of weather dynamics, they are all around us: a full 360 degrees. If the fireworks didn't imply the possibility of serious danger (masts, unfortunately, make good lightning rods), I'd sit back and enjoy the show, but I know there is no outrunning our entrapment, and the ensuing punishment. Sooner or later we will feel the effects of this pent-up power head-on.

And so it is. At the stroke of 10 p.m., the wind begins to blow erratically at an aggressive forty-five knots, turning the sea into a frothy, angry milkshake. We are tossed every which way while attempting to hold together in our first real-time test of boat and crew. It is tough going and downright scary, especially in the dark, which has a way of bringing out the fear goblins. If I didn't know better, I'd think we were on a rollercoaster, ready at any minute to shake loose from the stabilizing structure and spin completely out of control.

Then, in less than half an hour, all is calm again. It feels like the aftermath of a fight between lovers that flares up unpredictably, only to be transformed into sweet loving gestures after a quick, sexual union. There were the inevitable miscalculations during the storm, including dropping the mainsail too slowly, which necessitated a trip by Brett partially up the mast under high wind and rain to free the snagged sail. But our performance as a team was good, especially since this was our first real threat. I'm feeling grateful for the complementary skills of our crew (you wouldn't see me up the mast in those conditions). And *Kairos* took the ride like a champ, never flinching.

There are plenty of other opportunities to test our strength and unity as a crew, including a few before entering the ocean. Besides weather-related challenges, we experience several mechanical breakdowns. None of them prove catastrophic, but several shine a light on my still-developing capacity to trust in the universe.

At the start of the trip, after downing our celebratory glasses of champagne and before even leaving the dock, the engine overheats, which necessitates an additional full day of repairs. Talk about deflating. The upside is another bottle of champagne. The following day, when we are already five miles north of the port of exit, in the Atlantic and feeling optimistic, we have to turn back due to leaky oil hoses. Another day of repairs. Once we are finally underway, the fifty-pound radar unit falls off its mount at two in the morning, barely missing Evan. Power to the global positioning system is compromised, which means that we don't readily know with any degree of precision where we are (not an insignificant problem). The fuel line takes in air at three one morning, which requires "bleeding" the entire diesel system: a very messy and smelly job. Adding insult to injury, access to the fuel line is inconveniently located beneath my bunk, where I have been fast asleep getting some much-needed rest. And on it goes, part of traversing the ocean in a modern sailboat.

Amid the demanding push/pull of keeping the ship on course live my feelings for Evan. At times I remember him as a boy just learning to sail and answering his many questions, especially those related to rigging and navigation. I also recall, fondly, chewing him out numerous times for not washing the dishes after a meal. But I snap out of that reverie when the radar topples and almost hits him, now seeing the son who responds like a man with quick reflexes and a cool demeanor. In my mind, time expands and collapses around him—he smells of his mother's shampoo one moment, and then of beer the next. He talks of Updike and the relevance of place and space in our lives. He is both abstract and concrete, boy and man. Above all I feel blessed to know him, and to think that I may have had some small part to play in the shaping of this marvelous being.

"Fish up" yells Evan.

I am at the helm, motoring lazily along under the spell of the Gulf Stream, approximately seventy-five miles off the coast of Georgia. The wind is dead calm and the sea flat as the unanticipated excitement strikes hard, and fast. Prompted by the sport fishing boats that surround us, Evan and Brett had decided to try their luck at snagging a live one. We have a rather small rod and reel on board, something Evan and I used when he was a child for catching lake sunfish. In contrast, Brett brought along a big fish lure. Despite the incongruity of small pole/big lure, they rigged it up and tossed the line overboard, propelled with a wish and a prayer.

Within a few seconds of Evan's alert, it's obvious that there is a very large and colorful fish on the other end of the line. The swift being darts about frantically, trying to free itself from the grip of these two amateur, but motivated, fishermen. I surely think this story will end in disappointment, with the powerful fish breaking the line, the pole, both hearts, and most likely all of the above.

But Evan and Brett are determined to create a happy ending—for themselves at least. Rather than fight the fish directly, under Brett's coaching Evan allows the fish to tire by offering endless amounts of line. Meanwhile, the big fish keeps swimming hard in an intense effort to break free.

Every few minutes the fish Brett identifies as a mahi-mahi bolts rapidly from the boat at a ninety-degree angle, and then jumps high into the air, creating a truly spectacular sight. The colors of the fish's scales are iridescent yellow and blue, which add to the exciting visual display. Miraculously, the gear holds. After forty-five minutes of this, with my fishing duo showing no signs of fatigue, the magnificent creature makes the fatal mistake of swimming slowly and very close to the boat. Right on cue, Brett grabs the large gaff hook we have on board and snags the flashy fish, pulling it quickly onto the deck—all fifty pounds of it.

What follows is something you really have to see to believe. The mahi-mahi, which we later measure to be forty-one inches (just shy of 3.5 feet, nose to tail) is hell-bent on getting back into the water, and Brett shows equal perseverance in preventing that from happening. As the prize catch flaps wildly and gasps desperately for oxygen, Brett wrestles it to the deck. Both roll around frantically until Brett screams, "Alcohol. Need alcohol—now."

"You mean drinking alcohol?" I ask.

"Yes" he yells.

I quickly bring him a freshly opened beer, which he hastily pours into the gills of the fish (I think for a minute that it is for Brett, not the fish). Amazingly, the not-so-little creature gets immediately drunk and passes out. Fight over. Mission accomplished. All we have to do now is clean him up and get ready for the feast.

Fortunately, Brett is as good at dressing fish as he is at wrangling them. The now eternally peaceful mahi-mahi is swiftly cut up into twenty-seven portions (or nine meals each for the three of us), plus we all enjoy a little fresh sushi during the surgery. Then Evan, whose culinary sensibilities are quite refined, prepares an unforgettable dinner for us. You'd think we had just stumbled into a four-star restaurant in New York City, except that the view is infinitely more divine, and the fish a lot fresher. I can't tell if the better-equipped sport-fishing boats around us have been as successful that afternoon, but what Brett and Evan accomplish with our meager tools results in a well-deserved air of celebration and gratitude on *Kairos* that evening.

Prior to dinner, Brett and I start in with our usual dance around the invocation of grace. His blessings are decidedly Christian, mine heavily Buddhist. Both are filled with heart, but there is also a growing edge of competition between us as the offerings expand in length and complexity.

"So whose turn is it tonight?" I ask.

"Yours," says Brett, seeming relieved.

I sit back, get comfortable, and seek guidance. But none comes.

Instead, surprising myself and the others, I look at Evan and say, "Okay, bud, it's your turn."

Never one to shy from a challenge, Evan, reclining into his cockpit seat, eyes the wonderful dinner begging to be eaten and says, "Well, I think we've had enough words on this trip. Let's all just observe a bit of silence together."

Perfect I think, feeling humbled and proud. How does he know that is precisely what we need?

Feeling fully content, after delighting in a sumptuous meal, we finish the bottle of wine and the stories, ending the evening appropriately with a three-way hug. *Does it get any better for a dad?* I wonder.

Then—putt, putt, spurt, spurt ... silence.

Deep silence.

Glances all around.

The engine dies. Brett immediately goes below to assess the situation. A few minutes later he surfaces with the news.

"This is not a good scenario, guys. The raw water pump that keeps the engine cool is, well, kaput. And worse, we don't have the appropriate spare part to fix it. Plus, there is collateral damage. The generator, which is our back-up source to keep the batteries charged, is also down for the count. So we will be completely out of power in about twenty-four hours."

"Ugh," I mutter. "What to do now?" Normally the solution to the problem would be obvious—do what sailors have done for centuries without engine power: sail. But there is no wind, the sea is calm, and the batteries continue to deplete. Modern sailboats are, unfortunately, quite dependent on electrical power.

After only a few moments of ambivalence, I reach for the radio and suppress my embarrassment at asking for help. Thankfully, Tow Boat US (the AAA of the sea) responds immediately. After hearing a description of the problem, they assure us that a tow will be provided. Fortunately we are only twenty-five miles from Beaufort, NC, one of the best-equipped yachting centers on the East Coast, an excellent place to be close to if you need repairs. Under Brett's encouragement, and with some resistance from me, I signed up for the towing service only days before leaving

Florida. *The guides upstairs seem to be working overtime these days,* I note to myself.

It is well after midnight by the time our boat lines meet the dock. I hadn't wanted to surrender by calling in for help, but overall I am relieved. The towboat driver checks my membership, which cost me approximately $160, and goes on his way. Before leaving, I ask him what the charge would have been without having joined.

"Well, somewhere between eight and ten thousand dollars," he replies.

Sometimes it pays to have insurance, I think with a smile on my face. We all sleep well that night after having been out in the often stressful Atlantic for over one hundred hours. Being predictably safe and secure for a night, and not having to assume my 3 a.m. shift, feels just fine to me.

While the crew as a whole is holding together quite well, Captain Brett and owner Ed are beginning to experience some difficulties. Normally there is no democracy on a boat. The captain always has the last word, which appropriately unites responsibility and authority in one person, and makes for a clear chain of command. But it is my boat, and I also have a good deal of experience under my belt (probably too much of it managerial). Occasionally—and especially under tense conditions—captain and owner disagree, and sometimes we even clash.

Brett wants every detail explained in a highly linear and concrete manner, which is what makes him an excellent mechanic. I prefer responding intuitively, which is what makes me a good futuristic thinker. He goes for the details, while I push for the big picture. For many of us, this dynamic or some variation of it rings true on land (sound familiar?). But a few hundred miles out at sea, we don't have the luxury of going to opposite ends of the house, getting a good night's sleep, and working it out in the morning when fresh.

"Don't you think it's time to raise the sails, Brett?" I offer. We are departing Beaufort after successfully attending to the necessary engine repairs. The wind is howling at an impressive thirty-five knots, and I know we need to set the canvas now while we are still in the protected waters of the harbor.

His response is a terse, "No." He adds, "Too much traffic in here. I'd rather do it when we get out of the harbor."

But I know that won't happen. Unfortunately, I am proven right.

Exiting the harbor, the powerful wind is blowing hard and strong, forcing tons of surf right at us. Eight-foot waves crash over the bow making for one hell of an uncomfortable ride, and taxing the newly repaired engine to its max. It takes us four hours of motoring (very slowly) against very strong opposing surf before we are able to alter our course and add those handy white sheets (*Kairos* is a sailboat, after all). Without the benefit of sails in those first four hours—which would have helped significantly in adding both propulsion and stability—the ride is ugly and dangerous. I vow to be more assertive next time.

Despite the occasional tension between us, I like Brett and admire his talents, and from all indications, I believe the admiration is mutual. While I lack the patience for detail required to address many mechanical issues, Brett is less adept with the intuitive "wrap around" necessary for efficient strategic decisions. I know instinctually which destination is the most likely choice, and then go about testing analytically the integrity of that hunch. In contrast, Brett prefers to test the analytics on a half dozen or so possible options to see which one emerges a winner.

We move in contrary motion, but we work it out, and in the end respect each other for the complementary nature of our contributions—well, most of the time. Yes, relationship issues show up everywhere—perhaps especially out at sea among crew members. Good practice, since this is a limited engagement, and one we can walk away from in a few days. *All part of sailing from one place to another, both literally and metaphorically,* I think.

We sail on, moving gradually past the southern states while maintaining our maximum speed of six knots. On day seven we finally progress into the northern half of the American Atlantic, inching carefully around feared Cape Hatteras, North Carolina. Then we head straight north.

Days run into nights run into days, all passing silently as I allow myself to be lulled into an exceptional state of bliss. Living on *Kairos* round the clock in the middle of the Atlantic is a uniquely profound experience, I'm finding, one that flows from a close and developing intimacy with the natural elements—a continuous meditation on merging with the power and beauty of endless sky, water, and wind.

There is plenty of romance as well as we ride the ocean 24/7. The dolphins (ah, such elegant beings) become our friends, offering frequent visits as we watch and applaud their joyful play. Flying fish leap over and occasionally onto *Kairos*, while abundant species of birds—even butterflies—fly all about us. There are magnificent sunrises, sunsets, moonrises, and moonsets; gorgeous blue, blue, and more blue from both water and sky in every direction; and an almost mystical solitude, especially when one is alone on watch. My favorite time is deep into the night

> *... living on the water is an essential part of my transformation into a way of being that embraces impermanence as the natural way of things.*

with a full moon. The intense light illuminates the surf, creating a beautiful phosphorescent white skirt for *Kairos*. That same surf emits a deeply soothing sound as we glide along gracefully on nothing but wind power.

Gone is the anxiety I felt when leaving Cocoa. In this ocean of emptiness, I develop a deep sense of peace without need for artificial structures or anything that offers me a false sense of permanence. With the fluidity of water surrounding me, I too become absorbed in the great flow, perfectly content to hang out and just be. Had we the capacity on board for endless food and fuel, it feels like I could continue this sail forever.

Above all, the sail north confirms my instinct that living on the water is an essential part of my transition into the final third, and my transformation into a way of being that embraces impermanence as the natural way of things. I have learned that attempting to hold onto anything is an illusion, since the very nature of life is change. Just like the ocean, my latest, and best, teacher.

Tashmoo

9

Alone Again

Brett and I drop Evan off on the New Jersey coast so that he can catch a bus back to NYC, his summer home. Meanwhile, we head out northeast for the final thirty-six hours. The trip finale takes us initially south of Long Island, New York and then within ten miles of the spectacular southern cliffs on Block Island, Rhode Island. Finally we pull into Menemsha Harbor on Martha's Vineyard, Massachusetts, the summer resting place for *Kairos*, and thus the con-

Will I ever learn to trust more fully in the way of things?

clusion of our sail north. *Kairos*'s maiden voyage has taken a total of twelve and a half days, only two more than a straight shot. All things considered, it was a successful shakedown cruise.

But where there is light, there is shadow. Severing the connection with Evan happened much too fast. For ten days we were glued together hour after hour, sharing in strategic decisions, food preparation, sail trim, and other tactical responsibilities. Then suddenly he's gone. I haven't prepared myself, and I now miss him terribly.

It is the second week in July, and, despite my heavy heart, the fun summer weather is finally here. June has been unusually wet and dreary up north, so the timing of our trip, and the extended stay in Cocoa that caused it, now seem well-timed. I wonder, *Did the universe intentionally orchestrate my delay in Florida by stalling work on the boat?* What seemed to me like a royal screw-up at the time now appears as great good fortune. Will I ever learn to trust more fully in the way of things?

Brett and I stay only long enough at the small, quaint fishing village of Menemsha to fuel up. We then head back out to Vineyard Sound, the body of water approximately three miles wide by ten miles long. This well-navigated passageway separates the Vineyard and the Elizabeth Islands—a very beautiful string of island pearls with an equally alluring cache of names: Cuttyhunk, Nashon, Nashawena, and Pasque. As we sail up the Sound, I feel held by the comfort of familiarity, and the enveloping warmth of a clear summer day.

In every direction we see impressive homes, spectacular cliffs, and interesting seascapes of varying types, all displaying a full palette of colors. *How different from the preceding days on the ocean,* I think, where the views were filled with endless vistas painted in different shades of blue. For me, being back close to land is like seeing a rainbow for the first time. Somehow life just wants to be lived in contrasts; too much of anything, no matter what it is, eventually needs relief. Even rainbows.

Besides experiencing a dramatic visual shift, it is also reassuring to be sailing in protected waters again. We are on the lee side of a large island that stands between *Kairos* and the ocean. It feels like a wholly different sailing experience than the expansive and more wildly expressive ocean we were immersed in. I've sailed up Vineyard Sound many times, but that day was the sweetest, signaling the fulfillment of an important life dream of sailing the East Coast of America.

At the other end of the Sound is the entrance to Lake Tashmoo, my favorite harbor in all of Southern New England (SNE). It is reverentially quiet, gorgeous—even mysterious.

July and August in SNE can be tough going if what you are looking for is a remote place to hang out. The harbors are usually crowded with boaters who look forward to early and extended happy hours. There are not a lot of serious sailors in this neighborhood searching for peace, quiet, and—dare I say—solitude. Tashmoo is the exception.

I have typically sailed Maine in the summer months. It is the other extreme from SNE with its many choices for tranquil anchorages and folks who are, for the most part, looking to commune with the natural surroundings. But after a 1400 nautical-mile trip, I am not up for another two hundred mile hike up to Maine. Besides, I've promised many of my friends a visit on my new sea home,

Somehow life just wants to be lived in contrasts; too much of anything, no matter what it is, eventually needs relief. Even rainbows.

and I am eager to reconnect with them after having been away since mid-May. So, Tashmoo on the Vineyard is my harbor of choice for this summer.

"Lake" Tashmoo was once freshwater. I'm not sure when the town opened it up to Vineyard Sound, thereby making it a saltwater harbor and giving ocean-going yachters like me access to this nautical jewel, but I'm sure glad they did. Once inside a rather narrow and treacherous human-made inlet, whose navigation is restricted to locals and the fearless, the lake opens up, proudly displaying its rich visual splendor.

It is pear-shaped, surprisingly well-protected from winds, and offers numerous idyllic places to drop anchor. Spring, summer, or fall, its crown of leafed-out mature hardwoods provides an ever-changing visual greeting. At the southern end, opposite from the inlet and about two miles due south is a sweet, pond-like coda. Here the water fowl–Canadian geese, flying wild turkey, mallard duck, and an occasional swan—own the real estate, but will occasionally yield to humans if we behave with dignity and respect for the year-round occupants. Beauty and stillness dominate. The balance of nature feels aligned. This is one spot that tempts me to believe that there are concentrated pockets of energy on the earth's surface where the inexplicable happens.

As we enter Tashmoo from Vineyard Sound, I call upon my spiritual guides for help. Only with fortune on our side, will there be a rare vacant mooring waiting for us to snuggle up to. Motoring slowly, and expectantly, we inch closer to the far end of the lake. Then, almost like magic, there it is. Picking up the pendant, I let out a long deep breath, realizing that the universe has provided me with a private and deeply spiritual place to moor my sea home, and my soul. Throughout the summer and fall, leaving frequently and sometimes for extended periods, that same mooring is always magically available.

Brett will stay another few days to finish needed repairs before I reluctantly see him off for his flight back to Florida. Over the last several months we have developed a close friendship. Without Evan around, and without having to devote our concentration to sailing round the clock, we discover the luxury and challenge of deep conversation, most of it about fathers and sons.

Late one afternoon as we finish tightening the wheel mount, Brett says in his twangy Floridian accent, "I like the way you and Evan are. Ya know Ed, life with my dad was really hard. Growing up, all I heard was, 'Brett, can't you be more like me?'" He pauses, looks at me, and continues in his father's voice. "You'll never amount to anything fiddling around with gadgets. People get paid for their ideas, boy. That's where it's at."

I want to interrupt him and affirm what a great person he is, but he needs to keep going. Instead I open the wine.

ED MERCK

"'Forget the motors and hit the books,' he kept telling me. I never felt respected for who I was, and it's taken me years to really believe that my talents are worth anything."

"Funny thing," I say, nodding and passing him a glass. "The code for intelligence in my family was the ability to work with your hands. The world of ideas was seen as a place where the inept would hide if they couldn't make it doing *real* work." We clink glasses. "My father's favorite put-down was, 'Son, you have no common sense.' Only once did I find the courage to say, 'Dad, common sense is what you have and the other guy doesn't—it's not an absolute.' My father's dismissive shrug seemed to say, 'Well, that confirms what I just said.'"

Brett and I gradually realize that the attraction and the struggle between us come from the fact that I remind Brett of his father, and he reminds me of mine. When I get restless with his step-wise thinking, and he gets impatient with my lack of precision, we both feel underappreciated—filled with shadows from the past. These mirror images turn out to be very useful in unlocking some of the conflict we've had with one another, and within ourselves. Held by the magic of Tashmoo, we experience the strong union that has grown out of our differences (I hope both fathers are watching). Unknowingly throughout our several month association, we have been working on healing our father-wounds. With the help of good wine and spacious evenings, now is our time to make sense of it all.

Of course we both have sons of our own and have devoted much of our lives to ensuring that the stains of our fathers will not be repeated, but in doing so we have likely created new issues for our offspring by being the over-compensating sons of difficult fathers. Does the compensatory nature of changing generations ever fully heal itself? Wait, wasn't my grandfather—my father's father—an inventor and a musician, an idea man all the way? Spooky. Years from now I'd like to listen in on the stories our sons tell about us. I wonder, *How will we fare?*

Brett leaves early in the morning. The overcast rainy weather matches my somber mood perfectly, and I'm still missing Evan. With the Captain gone, I'm now where I knew I would end up all along—alone. Since leaving Rhode Island in late May, I've been distracted with the busyness of first preparing *Kairos* for the trip, and then engaging in the trip itself. During that period there were people all around, especially Brett and Evan. But now it's just me, *Kairos*, and the pond at Tashmoo. I am caught unprepared. "Why didn't I see this coming?" I ask wistfully, knowing the answer but too embarrassed to admit it even to myself. This is supposed to be my dream, my pot of gold at the end of the rainbow, yet instead of holding treasure, I sit in the cockpit feeling the grayness of being alone. I even wonder if this whole adventure has been a colossal mistake.

My journey with aloneness began in earnest several years earlier when Catherine and I split up. In truth, I have always felt oddly different from the mainstream, seeking something I looked for desperately at times but could not find in our culture's implicit social contract. It often feels like I have a different set of honing devices than most people. Even the way I typically frame the struggles of humanity places me outside the 95% bracket (and I'm feeling generously inclusive at the moment).

Take war, for example. Do we really kill our own brothers and sisters for a set of ideals that stem from preserving the vested interests of powerful players? I know that if I found myself on the other side of a rice paddy with my sergeant screaming "Shoot," I'd have to think about it.

Would I kill someone to support religious ideas or economic interests? The whole thing seems bizarre to me, yet the majority of our population embraces war-making as a natural byproduct of statecraft and human nature. (For that matter, I think the organization of the globe into nation states has woefully outlived its usefulness.) Rather than shoot, I would likely put down the weapon, extend my hand, and say something like,

"This is madness, bro. Let's light a candle, create a meal together, talk heart-to-heart, and figure out a better way." I know it would work, which further certifies my anomalous nature.

I joined the National Guard Band in 1968 as a way of side-stepping a tour in Vietnam. Back then basic training combined recruits from the Guard and the Army, the folks who were soon headed to the other side of the world to shoot "bad guys" in their jungles, rice paddies, and tunnels. All this in the mythical name of preserving freedom.

One early morning, standing in battalion formation and wearing our full fatigues with weapons strapped to our shoulders, I whispered to my friend Tom standing beside me, "Hey, dig that sunrise, man. Pretty amazing, huh?"

He paused to look at the layers of intense color in the sky and said, "Yeah bro, thanks for noticing." He looked for a long time, then replied, "Thank God we take in things like this—saves me from going mad."

I grew to love Tom, especially during our special moments together, and I'll never reconcile how such a beautiful spirit could have drawn the war card. He was educated, refined, and from old southern gentry, but there he was, ready to put his life on the line for freedom, or whatever the political mantra was at that moment.

A year after basic training, I put through a call to Tom's home in Georgia. He should have been back from Nam by then, and I wanted to see how he made out. His father answered. After I introduced myself the phone fell silent. "Tom was killed," his father explained. "We had a service for him—I'm sorry to have to tell you."

I pictured his flag-draped casket being carried off the plane and lowered into the ground. Tears still well up in my eyes when I think of him and his fate. Is there really any decent way of justifying his death at twenty-two, especially when I went off to play John Phillips Sousa in the National Guard Band?

Having a minority view—and not just when it comes to war—has often led to my sense of isolation. I've found myself there many times, and it's a damn uncomfort-

> "As long as there are states of mind that I think cannot be tolerated, I will live behind bars."

able place to hang out. I've longed for the opposite, to feel more a part of the majority, however that manifests. Why can't I adopt a more conventional life? Why am I always searching for something beyond the norm, beyond the obvious? It would be so much easier, and a heck of a lot more fun, if I could accept the "American way of life" that is offered up to us by marketers who want us to think they are speaking for everyone.

For many years I avoided feelings of loneliness. It was too painful—much easier to distract myself with work and family responsibility. But after my divorce from Catherine, I finally began to address it head-on. It hasn't been pretty, but at least now I can utter the phrase "I am lonely" without flinching. Oddly enough, by looking loneliness in the eye it has taken on a softer quality—still uncomfortable at times, but without the sting.

Befriending loneliness has been a necessary step on my journey. Somehow I knew that making it to the other side of this transition would require a fuller reconciliation of my longing for connection, and a more comfortable fit with being alone. As one of my spiritual teachers is fond of saying, "As long as there are states of mind that I think cannot be tolerated, I will live behind bars." You might say I've spent the last ten years working my way closer to the exit door in the prison of my fears.

Several years back, acting on the guidance of another spiritual teacher, I took a week-long vacation on the water. My teacher offered little direction, only this: "Be on the water, alone, and with as few distractions as possible." Sailing a boat with the beautiful name *Namaste* (roughly translated: I honor the light within you), I moored in the pond at Tashmoo and stayed there for seven days. I did engage in activities like bike rides through the country and grocery shopping. But alone time was primarily focused on allowing my awareness to expand more deeply into the silence.

I used intentional techniques like meditation, breath work, and chanting; primarily, though, the exercise was to just *be*. To sit in my own experience and not try to fill it with anything, to become an acute observer of my ever-changing inner reality and all that was going on around me.

Moving increasingly into the world of my senses, I felt a universal connection to all around me. The geese that flew overhead every morning and evening, the tides that lifted the water, and thus my home up and down several feet twice a day, the trees and flowers that offered their beauty, the small fish that jumped to avoid the larger fish in pursuit, the infinite rich-

I am that conscious awareness.

ness of natural sounds like tree frogs and crickets, and those funny wild turkeys that spent the night up a tree—these all became part of my world, and part of me in a way that made loneliness impossible. I began to discover that not only was this conscious awareness all around me, but even more poignantly, I *am* that conscious awareness.

This is my work—the investment of life energy that will really count. And I know it will never end, but rather continue to deepen my connection to the ever-present stillness within. Toward the end of that week alone at Tashmoo, I felt drawn to answer a question that had taken form in my mind: *What is the deepest calling for my life?* Here is my spontaneous response, saved in a now-tattered notepad, most of which still speaks to me today:

Be open to the love that is inherent in all things, knowing with every cell in my body, mind, and spirit that I am part of this larger whole.

Allow this love to flow through me at all times, listen for its clues, and follow its direction.

Bring forgiveness and compassion to myself and then to others; avoid judging my past and future missteps; avoid seeking comfort only in people and ideas that limit my concept of myself and the universe; and love whole-heartedly.

Keep myself challenged on the path of growth while fully accepting my current state of awareness.

Yet, even with this wonderful lesson from the past, and years of practice in between, I am still feeling the morning grayness. Missing both Evan and Brett, I sit here in the open cockpit of *Kairos* eating breakfast. However in tune I have become over the years to the splendor of the nonhuman world around me, and however intensely and consistently I connect to the oneness of it all, I still need contact with others. *And that is okay* I tell myself, with only a hint of hesitation.

When I left Rhode Island six months ago, I made the choice to go it alone and face the inevitable consequences. It was not what I wanted, or how the ideal picture of my life looked in my mind's eye. In truth, I secretly hoped a sailing partner would emerge who would make my quest easier, who would still the longing in me. Yet despite the lack of an attractive first mate, I was determined to engage in this sea-adventure.

So I did, and I am occasionally lonely. *These are just feelings*, I tell myself, *not my whole being*. For now, it is better to let them be and not seek out a premature resolution. I want to remain in the mystery of not knowing, which is for me the most spiritual of places and, not surprisingly, the most difficult.

Sinking deeper into my seat with unfinished coffee in hand, I allow myself to further soften into these emotions. Gradually my resistance begins to diminish as a more optimistic mood emerges. The sun breaks through the mist, and I think again about the possibility of filling that vacant first mate slot. She sure looks good in my imagination.

As I toss off the mooring line for the day's sail, a spontaneous prayer emerges from my lips:

Open, oh place of pure awareness

And end my suffering from separation.

Satisfy my longing for connection

Alone, and in exile no more.

Kairos Down Below

10
Close Encounters of the Amorous Kind

I first sailed into Tashmoo over twenty-five years ago on a small eighteen-foot boat. Since then I've been called back many times. This occasion is particularly noteworthy, since it represents my first extended immersion into living on the water. Sure I'm looking forward to short sailing trips with friends, and there are plenty of repairs and upgrades to tend to on *Kairos*, but mostly I just want to settle in a bit. I want to find out what it is like living full-time on a boat. After all, that *is* the plan.

Kairos, my dear floating home, is an exceptional vessel. Only twelve years old, she is young enough to still feel new, but old enough to have most of the mechanical kinks worked out. Her pleasing exterior lines and classic appointments draw the attention of most. And, as if beauty isn't enough, she is also dependably seaworthy; a true ocean-going craft. Sailors often feel compelled to pause and offer comments like "Beautiful boat you have," their tones tinged with envy.

Kairos has a generously sized cockpit that features a canvas overhang called a bimini to shade from the sun; and a dodger, which redirects any strong wind around the outside. Overall this makes for a very pleasant open-air living room. There I can be found most days and nights engaged in eating, napping, exercising, meditating, reading, listening to music, or just sitting quietly in this cozy exterior space with water views at a full 360 degrees.

Down below, however, is the real reason for my love affair. The organization and detailing of the enclosed living space makes for a truly unique presentation. Most sailboat designs take whatever precious space there is and subdivide into small functional areas. Several months of living in tightly walled-off living quarters would have me screaming for escape.

In contrast, there is no feeling of claustrophobia on board *Kairos*. With the exception of an enclosed head, and a partially enclosed king-sized berth under the cockpit, the remainder of the area is one open room. This space then easily transforms into any number of uses, including dining, living, sleeping, cooking, and navigating. There is ample storage capacity around the edges—both the lying-flat closet type and the hanging-locker variety—that gives the entire interior the feel of permanency. Living out of duffle bags would get old real fast.

Most stunning is the finish—almost every surface covered in beautiful, high-grade cherry, which radiates warmth and soft reflected light. Spatially, the enclosed area feels twice as large as its actual dimensions would suggest. How did the designers pull off this perceptual trick? I'm still trying to figure that out, and smiling while I do.

Each of these areas is also well-equipped. The galley, for example, has a gas stove/oven that rivals any I've used on land, a generous sink with hot and cold running water, a microwave, an ice-maker, a desalinating water maker, and a full refrigeration unit with freezer. Not to mention plenty of storage space for food, dishes, utensils, etc. There is even an entertainment center with TV/DVD, a magnificent-sounding stereo with iPod hookup, and satellite radio. Who needs a land base?

As to transportation logistics, there is my trusty water taxi: a cute little ten-foot inflatable dinghy with four-horsepower engine hanging off the stern. It is available whenever I need a quick lift to shore or back. Once on land, despite the secluded nature of the mooring, access to food and most other supplies is a short walk away. Plus, if I feel in need of a bit of culture, an outdoor Shakespearian theatre is nearby whose 2009 repertoire includes *A Midsummer Night's Dream* and *The Taming of the Shrew*.

For exercise, my preferred options include walks to and from errands, cycling on my rented bike, or swims off the stern in the cleanest blue green water SNE has to offer. After a workout, I usually avail myself of the outdoor shower on *Kairos* to rinse off any salt and sand before I go below. I am not a sailor lacking the comforts of home.

Of course I occasionally sink back into that all-too-familiar place of loneliness. But for the most part, living on *Kairos* this summer has me feeling alive and buoyant, as if I'm back in my natural element after all those years of living on land, and yes, behind a desk. Without any effort I sleep better, have greater energy, exhibit stronger mental clarity, and feel more relaxed. My biological rhythms recalibrate to the soft water energy around me supporting a more peaceful and spirit filled connection to life force.

It certainly would be possible for me to hang out within one mile of moored *Kairos* all summer and be perfectly happy. But why do that when there are 87.5 square miles of beautiful island to enjoy? Moving around this jewel of a land mass is convenient as well, with a bus transportation system that crisscrosses the island in a sophisticated network consisting of thirteen interconnected routes. Plus I can easily get off the island by taking any one of several slow- and high-speed ferries that connect with different mainland locations. Even if I were inclined to have a car, it would be totally redundant.

I'm not sure who "Martha" was, but the virtues of the island named for her are many. Unlike many other islands I'm familiar with; her offerings are far from the typical monochromatic theme of beach, sand, and shops. There are actually six uniquely different towns, all held within a rich and diverse ecosystem. Here is a brief tour of what I reveled in throughout the summer and fall of 2009:

Vineyard Haven is where most island ferries dock, making it a central transportation hub and thus a bit of a tourist attraction. Occupying a prominent place in the working harbor, Martha's Vineyard Shipyard boasts a 150 year history of yacht restoration, and continues in that tradition today with expert repairs and superior ship building. Its Ship's Store, used often by me, is one of the finest in New England. For the more intellectually minded, Bunch of Grapes, called "One of the best little bookstores in America" by William Styron, offers as comprehensive and diverse a collection of books as can be found anywhere, all packaged in an imaginative and inviting bookish atmosphere. I often hang out there for hours at a time, especially on a rainy, inclement day.

A few miles east is Oak Bluffs. Here the tourist attractions have a bit more energy to them, likely due to the fact that unlike "dry" Vineyard Haven, alcohol is legal and abundantly available. There is a lot of bogie for every taste, with large marinas, colorful architecture, diverse and snappy restaurants, and a great beach that I use frequently to either stimulate my senses, calm my mind, or both. Its impressive domestic architecture consists of hundreds of imaginative and colorful gingerbread cottages, containing the most perfectly preserved collection of Carpenter Gothic style architecture in the world. And while I tend to avoid the hot spots, I do regularly enjoy both walking and biking through this fascinating historic neighborhood.

Immediately downtown is the Flying Horses Carousel, the nation's oldest operating platform carousel, which is a favorite of young children and grown kids. Evan, Catherine, and I spent many hours—sometimes days—here as a young family. Now

I pass by, watching the newcomer parents and longing for that experience again. Catherine and I were so proud of our little boy back then. He always ended the ride with a huge smile on his face and the brass ring in his hand, which earned him yet another go around on this magical spinning world. Now the magic lives on in my heart.

Heading southeast along famous and very spacious State Beach we eventually reach Edgartown, in my mind the most scrubbed down of the towns, offering a strong gravitational pull for the better financially endowed among us. From the yacht club to the pricey restaurants and inns to the swank shops offering every possible object, it is not a place to hang out if you have to ask the price. And so I mostly don't—hang out, that is.

Long, lazy walks are my pleasure in this beautiful location. It is also my choice for a special dinner with friends or an occasional date when I get lucky.

While not directly in the town center, Chappaquiddick Island (officially part of Edgartown and home to the infamous Kennedy late-night car ride) creates a sculptural masterpiece, blending sand dunes, beach grass, gorgeous homes, frontage on famed Nantucket Sound, and its own rich inventory of bays, ponds, and streams. Many an afternoon I find a vacant rocker on the porch of one of the posh inns and gaze out onto this splendid seascape.

Bearing west along Martha's private and highly exclusive south shore is West Tisbury, the island's center. Unlike Vineyard Haven, Oak Bluffs, and Edgartown, this community is not formed around a harbor with an accompanying rich nautical history. Instead—and very much in relief—this is an essentially agrarian template with plentiful farms, old-growth trees, a high ratio of livestock and wildlife to humans, and a general focus on the fruits of the land rather than the sea. I enjoy biking along the hilly and mostly car-free roads of this town, making frequent stops to enjoy beautiful landscapes, or staring down one of the steer-like creatures with the big horns for fun (if it is behind a secure fence, of course).

Every Wednesday and Saturday I make my way, carrying empty grocery bags, to the famous West Tisbury Farmer's Market, a combination of convention and circus. Here the town's most gifted farmers and craftspeople attractively display their offerings of food and handicrafts. It is hard to exaggerate the abundance I am greeted with upon entering this hallowed outdoor space. Vegetables of every imaginable size, shape, and color that are mostly organic and all local; prepared foods ready to eat; food condiments like jellies and sauces; and even organic meats all scream, "Look at me, take me home." An incredible dance ensues as the commingling of product and potential consumer energies combine to create an intense, energetic swirl. I find this twice-weekly ritual to be nothing short of bliss, and eminently practical as well.

If this all sounds rather sexy, it is. And here is a little secret—online dating venues are not the best option for connecting with interesting potential mates, the West Tisbury Farmer's Market is. Something about the overtly sensual nature of this place stimulates close encounters of the amorous kind. At least that is my experience. Try it—you'll like it.

Farther west is the town of Chilmark, topographically a close cousin to West Tisbury. With one notable exception, here too the agricultural flavor dominates. Invoking images of Vermont on an island, I enjoy biking and observing with delight the gentle rolling hills filled with roaming sheep, other livestock, flowers, and vegetables. I often stop in at one of the plentiful farm stands and purchase fruits of abundance directly from each land steward.

Menemsha, the island's fishing village, is the notable exception to the agrarian flavor of Chilmark. This is where Captain Brett and I made our landfall on the trip north. Still working today is a small but impressive fishing fleet of draggers and sport fishing craft. This collection of boats keeps two—yes, two—full-service fish markets well-stocked and busy with eager customers. Besides fish, I often purchase prepared lobsters, raw or cooked clams, soups, and other tantalizing sea-based foods. For eating, there are rustic tables out back fronting the harbor with a great view.

Perhaps the most impressive natural feature of Menemsha is the beach, which faces northwest (where the sun goes down in the summer). This is a favorite place of mine and hundreds of other summer hobos. Closing my eyes, I can hear the collective cheer that hails the setting sun on a clear night, and I can feel the sense of community that emerges from a shared sense of awe.

On the west side of Menemsha Harbor is the bike ferry (yes, you can't get on without a bike). A short trip across the inlet brings us to Aquinnah, the final township of this virtual tour. The most spectacular feature of Aquinnah is the cliffs at Gay Head, which define the western tip of the island. Featured are incredible water views in three directions atop the majestic and multicolor bluffs, formed with red, black, gray, white, and yellow clay deposits left over from the last ice age some ten-thousand years ago. Gay Head and much of the property in Aquinnah is owned by the Wampanoag Native American tribe, the largest collection of Native Americans in Massachusetts. Gracing the cliffs is a most noble lighthouse, originally opened in 1799. This landmark still beams white and red light to help mariners navigate up or down Vineyard Sound. On a sunny day, I love to take a nap at the base of this historical hot spot and dream of mariners past—perhaps even me in a prior lifetime.

On one relatively small island I have access to unsurpassed beauty, availability of every imaginable good and service, unparalleled diversity of ecological and human-inhabited environments, and convenient transportation. What more could a guy ask for? Well, how about friends?

Fortunately I have a rich array of them, who seem eager to reconnect after my four months' absence. Of course, it doesn't hurt that they seem curious to observe firsthand how their bud Ed is faring in his new adventure. Going out for a sail on an ideal summer day turns out to be an incentive as well. Making contact with these friends is helped by a rogue wireless signal that I can access on my laptop directly from the boat—another mysterious gift of this delightful mooring in Tashmoo.

My favorite visits are the extended ones. Taking off for a few days while leisurely exploring the abundant riches of life on the water works just fine for me. The most stress we experience is being treated to postcard-perfect harbors, abundant and very fresh seafood sometimes caught off the boat, frequent dips in the ocean, or extended conversations over a glass of wine or beer.

Several of these three-to-four-day sailing trips have been with two of my favorite female friends. Prior to this, our friendships had been restricted to enjoying a meal together, good conversation, and long walks. But now, due to the uniqueness of a boat, we are able to spend time round the clock.

Tish, roughly my age and a respectable big-time money manager when she's not off sailing with her kooky friend (me), insists every evening on converting the living room couch into the full queen-sized berth. She also prefers to erect the temporary wall that creates the effect on *Kairos* of a separate state room. Privacy is the message here.

On the other hand, my former employer Melissa—yoga studio owner/teacher and about fifteen years my junior—could care less about the separating wall or a queen-sized berth. When it's time to sleep, she just pulls out her sleeping bag and snuggles up on part of the living room couch. Meanwhile, I stay in the aft berth with the door shut. Carefree living is the message here.

Morning routines for both women are also vastly different, as are their food preferences, nap times, appetite for being alone, and choice of topics for discussion. It's truly fascinating to observe their variations up close, like being afforded entry into their secret lives.

I thoroughly enjoy both trips, and they reaffirm the desirability of platonic friendships. I'm not sure how the energy works but for me, when there is no sexual component to a relationship, or deep vulnerability that often flows from physical intimacy, the nature of the dance seems wildly different. Actually not so wild, and often more honest, free-flowing, and intimate in its own right.

With platonic love however, my friends and I seem to go into "The Love" together, a more spiritual place that feels free and connective at the same time.

Romantic love often finds me falling "in love" with a person, as if they are the vessel through which I can open to love. From that dynamic sometimes flows the trap of attachment and its ugly cousins: jealously, obsession, and desire. With platonic love however, my friends and I seem to go into "The Love" together, a more spiritual place that feels free and connective at the same time. I truly cherish these adventures with my female friends; they are unique experiences I think cannot be replicated with my guy friends, or perhaps even with a lover.

It doesn't escape me, however, that my spin on this relationship dynamic likely signals some aversion to deep closeness. I've had this awareness for a while, especially while watching many of my romantic connections implode, with me usually running for the exit door. Is the shelter of platonic love really more desirable? Maybe I should stick with sailing; I know I can do that.

Sailor Ed

11
Romance

Suddenly the universe throws me a curve ball. Romance—what else. Into the void the energy shall flow. And flow it does, with abundance and sweet abandon. Ah, my attractive, cuddly, hellcat Samantha. But I'm getting ahead of myself.

It's now been almost ten years since my separation from Catherine. In the interim we've remained on good terms, communicating when necessary about anything to do with Evan. As for staying married back then, we had in my opinion moved beyond each other's grasp, and were no longer interested in doing the hard work necessary to redesign our life together. She was seventeen years younger than me—an age spread that worked when we were both primarily consumed with work and parenting. But as I moved into the final third with greater concern for developing an inner life, and she towards a solidification of her career, our paths diverged.

After the marriage dissolved, I gradually reentered the shark-filled singles' pool. And it hasn't always been a pretty sight. Except for one five-year relationship, my track record with women over the last decade looks more like a string of volcanic explosions. My astrologer friend blames it on the heavenly bodies, at least as they manifest in me. With Pluto sitting right on top of "my" Venus, I apparently view relationships as a means to foster transformation. Not an easy cosmology to cope with, for either partner. It makes for lots of personal growth, yet often rocky times together.

For at least five of the past ten years I've participated in an online dating service that caters to a "green" clientele. *Better than bars* I tell myself. And it saves time by screening for folks with similar values: spiritual and ecologically minded. There they are—hundreds of available women, photos and written profiles included, and all looking for the same thing—companionship and romance. At first it felt like I had fallen into a candy store with no limits on consumption. *Was it really going to be that easy,* I wondered?

Well, "easy" isn't the adjective I'd choose. Fun, exciting, stimulating, and provocative, yes, but not easy. Over the years, I engaged in quite a few "skirmishes," but none of them made it to the sustainable category. They (we) always looked good on paper—or in this case, online—but the longer-term reality wasn't quite as satisfying. It seems that the electronic medium is good at providing options, but not at protecting against a broken heart. Despite the pain, I've remained an eternal optimist, continuing to believe that "The One" will emerge, and soon.

Enter Samantha, right on cue. Our connection began while I was still in Cocoa, waiting for *Kairos* to be ready for the sail north. Here was a woman in New Hampshire thinking she was contacting a guy in Rhode Island, who in fact was about to move onto a sailing vessel in Florida. When the email inquiry arrived, I almost ignored it. To be sure, I've wondered many times since how life would have been different if I had.

I was acutely aware of how distracting and even dangerous female energy can be, especially if I wanted to stay on track with my transition from land to sea. The temptation to reply however was too great, especially as I soon realized through her emails that she was culturally sophisticated, widely read, and extremely articulate. Besides which, her pictures showed her to be bright-eyed, blonde, and a little wild. I have come to think "feral" is a more apt description, but how could I have known then?

We continued to exchange emails—mostly informational, but always with a flirtatious edge to them. Whether by design or by nature, she worked her spell on me through the electronic ether. I explained my situation, and we agreed that I would call her after I arrived back in New England with *Kairos*.

The phone number she gave me two months earlier works, but my initial try yields only the message machine. Sometimes technology can come in handy, since I am able to check out her voice print before having to fully engage. Listening to her message tells me she is strong, upbeat, even alluring. I sit back and wait for the return call, assuming there will even be one.

"Hi, this is Samantha," she offers in a sweet, mellifluous tone. "Thanks for the call. I've been wondering where you were and if you'd call."

"Yeah, nice to hear your voice," I say, inwardly embarrassed to feel how compelling it is to make contact. "You sound sweet, even gentle."

"Well, don't let that distract you too much—I can also turn up the volume when I need to," she says with a kind of breathy suggestiveness.

"I like your energy," I say, chuckling. "I can hear the thrust in your voice, but the edges are rounded." I can't believe the steam I'm feeling from her already.

"Yes, sweet yet forceful, that's me." She could be reading the telephone book—I am hooked by her voice already, no matter what she is saying.

Putting down the phone, I can smell the possibility of danger. It wouldn't be the first time I've been tempted to reach for the flame, only to be scalded. I can tell from this brief phone exchange that here is a fire goddess. Don't I need this time alone in Tashmoo to deepen my skills of awareness and self-reflection?

Isn't solitude my true teacher, my down payment toward an easier transition into the final third?

Yes, solitude is my teacher, but Eros gets me going.

Call number two: "Ed, I've missed you since we last talked."

I answer, chewing a muffin. "Hang on," I say, barely able to talk. "A muffin—"

"Golden raisin with saffron?" she offers. "No trans fats?"

I try swallowing, but my throat's not cooperating. Finally, "No, but sounds good."

"I hope you like to cook because I like to eat," she says, "but in my kitchen I can be very demanding."

I will later come to know what she means by that, but in this moment I want to be in her kitchen eating saffron threads from her fingers. I say, "I'm sure we'd be compatible in the kitchen."

To which she adds, "And in other rooms of the house, I hope."

From there she goes on to talk about a piece of fiction in a recent issue of *The New Yorker,* and her thoughts on picnics and the history of lunch in the wild. She paints pictures I want to insert myself into. She is charming, intricate, and complex.

Call number three: "Hi Ed, thanks for your message. Would love to visit you in Tashmoo—the name alone tells me much about you."

"I'm glad. Let's see if we can find a time."

"Next weekend?" she asks, without a speck of hesitation.

"Sure, and we'll work out the details—I mean about comfort, food, and … sleeping arrangements. I mean you could stay at—"

"Doesn't your boat have places to sleep? *Kairos,* the place of opportunity?" she says gently while giggling. "Such a boat must have many possibilities."

And so we launch our plan. The dance has begun, and this one feels like it has the potential of a slow, sexy waltz laced with all the excitement of highly coordinated twists and turns. *It's all about energy*, I think after we hang up. This budding connection certainly stimulates my energetic juices. Yet I also know that email and phone contact can afford you a peek behind the curtain, but the real test is how it plays out in person. *We shall see*, I say to myself, feeling a slight echo of disbelief in my heart.

Om Shanti

12
Second Thoughts

It is late morning on a gorgeous sunny Saturday when the ferry with mystery woman aboard appears in the distance. My senses are on high alert as I intuit the potential life-altering nature of the next few days. Staying in the moment seems almost impossible as my mind races through myriad scenarios. Am I really about to spend three full days on *Kairos* with a woman I've never met? I seldom worry about deodorant failure, but the concept suddenly crosses my mind.

No sooner has the ferry docked when off steps a sprightly blonde with radiant energy gazing in my direction. As we approach one another, it is clear we have to hug. Slim, firm in my arms. A brief touch of cheeks. "Hello, Samantha I presume."

"Oh, I thought you were from the Chamber of Commerce," she says, grabbing her backpack and half-leading us off the dock. "Very friendly place."

"Yes, we greet all our lovely visitors in this manner," I say, feeling the hard muscles in her arm. Then I overhear myself say to her, "I can do this."

And she immediately replies, "You bet we can." Good God, the energy is pouring out of her. *Thank goodness I am here to catch it*, I think.

We are off and running at a pace that feels like just under a four-minute mile. Within moments our bodies are "accidentally" brushing up against each other, which leads to holding hands on the bus ride to Tashmoo. Once at the lake, I take every opportunity to wow her. We walk hand in hand though the flower-filled nature preserve, then past the herring ladder with new life brimming over, all en-route to the dinghy that will speed us out to beautiful *Kairos*.

Stepping out of the small inflatable and onto the boat, Samantha says, "We are blessed to be held in the beauty and the light of this moment." She then sprinkles dried pink rose petals throughout the cockpit as an offering (I'm not kidding—she really does this).

It is love at first sight—I mean, between Samantha and *Kairos*. Of course it doesn't hurt my case any. Settling in fast, we immediately go for a swim. She looks gorgeous in her blue bikini, with jagged yellows and reds shot through it. We hop up on the deck and shower to take off the salt. She laughs with delight as the warm water hits her. I like the shower too, but seeing it through her eyes gives it new life, as many things will in the days to come.

We then speed over to the beach as the sun begins to catch up with the horizon across Vineyard Sound. Before leaving the boat, Samantha slips into a soft, formfitting black cotton dress that captivates me and deepens my breathing. *Who needs yoga with a tempestuous soprano like Samantha?* I think, as I feel myself being sucked ever deeper.

Back to the boat for wine and appetizers, I offer Samantha a hearty Merlot along with the best runny goat cheese on the island. Together we watch a magnificent sunset from the same side of the cockpit, while the geese overhead make their final flights of the day, honking wildly with approval. I've planned a magnificent meal to follow, but…well, let's just say we end up saving the food for another day. The attraction is so enticing, and at so many levels, that I am not about to refocus my attention from scintillating connection to the logistics of preparing a meal. Now what were those questions I'd been asking myself a few days prior about the dangers of being distracted from my spiritual path?

The remainder of the weekend follows the same upbeat tempo. We enjoy more swimming, cooking, sailing, rich conversation, and many other activities, including a trip to the previously mentioned West Tisbury Farmer's market. I love the way I feel being with her—she brings out the vertical dimension in an otherwise polyphonic me. And I revel in the way Samantha playfully engages the local vendors, flying around the fairgrounds in her lacy raspberry-colored dress as she samples the fruits of the vendors' labor. I am in a swirl, unable and unwilling to distinguish between the fragrant lilies she touches, the juicy berries she eats, or the sensuality she oozes. I only learn later that underneath her beautifully flowing dress was—well, nothing.

Even though I am for the moment along for the ride—okay, fully complicit in the ride—I can sense danger behind this much amperage. Will the heat burn itself out, or will there be something sustainable here? There is no question I find her overt desire irresistible. At the same time, the mariner in me hears—yet ignores—the life-saving sound of the clanging buoy.

Our pheromones like each other a lot, and the conversation on a wide array of subjects flows easily. She loves technology and graphics, European history and cooking, music from Louisiana, and dinosaurs. All weekend I experience the intoxicating rush of two energies blending: Samantha's feminine, my masculine; her proclivity for extroversion, mine for introversion. I feel bigger, lighter, and more expanded than usual. I am the sum of all those elements, like being on steroids.

"A potpourri of ideas and tastes, a mix-and-match girl, that's me," she says with a sparkle that, while endearing and stimulating, seems slightly rehearsed. Instead of heeding the warning signs though, I succumb to arousal. The mating dance, with all its fire and complexity, is well-choreographed, as if the heavens are rooting for this woman. Cupid's arrows are hitting their mark square on.

Her parting comment upon stepping off of *Kairos* and onto the dock at weekend's close is, "Okay, when I get home I'm going to notify all those other suitors on the dating service that my prince has come. Then I'll cancel my membership."

"And what about you?" she asks, staring pointedly into my eyes.

"Uh, yeah, me too," I reply, feeling both attracted to, and just a bit overwhelmed by the boldness of her delivery.

As if that isn't enough, when the taxi bringing Samantha back to the ferry pulls away from the curb, she opens the window and throws me a present, saying, "Hey Ed, here, these are for you. And don't wash them." I look down, and in my hands are her light-green lace panties. Trying to regain my balance from such a forceful volley, I stretch the elastic and place it over my head like a chef in a 4 XXXX restaurant, waving goodbye with a big grin on my face.

Back on *Kairos* with the scented trophy firmly in hand, my self-inquiry begins rapid fire. No question about the passion, but what of the subtler feelings that make for a good match? How would she be in a pinch? Does she have empathy for others? She plays well, but does she see people as toys for her own amusement? Is there really room in her life for ME—the real me, not just her projections? Most importantly, could I disintegrate in her fire?

I suppose there are worse ways to go. And, in the short term I don't want to forget about the practical aspects of compatibility like financial resources, children, grandchildren, and other significant commitments of time for work and community. God, I'm jumping ahead, but do I really think that she is willing and/or able to drop all and come sail away with me? What future life scenario does she have in mind? What are the potential deal-breakers for her?

And even if joining me is ultimately her choice, I'm acutely aware of my vulnerability around wanting a sailing mate. How much of me am I willing to mortgage in order to complete the perfect picture of a couple sailing off into the sunset?

Besides, experience teaches me that first encounters, however favorable, are not necessarily good indicators of long-term results. The nature of chemistry is clear and immediate: it's either there or it isn't. But long-term compatibility enjoys taking its time before manifesting any clues, much less any certainty.

The phone rings in the midst of my musings. I can hear it but can't see it. Finally, I find the phone in one of my bags. It's Samantha, but she's hung up. I dial her back. No answer. "Samantha hi, this is Ed, sorry to have missed your call—heard you ringing but couldn't reach you in time. Call back. And thanks for all that, I mean the weekend…bye." I put the phone on the galley top as I open the access door to the engine. Our last time out the engine was hard to start—I figure the fuel filter is getting clogged.

Soon my hands are covered in diesel, and the phone rings. "Shit," I mutter as I pull myself away and head for the phone while reaching for a paper towel. With only one clean hand the phone goes silent. Looking down I see that it's Samantha again. I call her back and she doesn't answer. As I sit for a moment waiting for her call, I'm wondering if it's the cosmos speaking. We have the illusion of connection, but when we pick up the phone, neither of us is there. After a while I go back to my repairs with the phone stationed where I can grab it, but she doesn't call back. At least the fuel filter gets replaced.

Falling into a book by Ram Dass entitled (appropriately) *Still Here Now*, I stretch out in this comfy way I have of arranging the pillows in the cockpit with the water at my feet and nature all around me.

The phone rings. "Ed, there you are. Where were you? I called and each time you hung up—what happened?" Then noticeably raising the volume in her voice, "What were you doing? I was on the side of the road, that horrible Route 6 with cars whizzing. I call you for help, and you hang up." She's now breathless on top of angry.

Blindsided, I respond, "I couldn't find the phone, and when you called again—"

"I got a flat tire somewhere. I think it was that funky town—I don't know; Falmouth maybe—and I pulled over and felt awful. My mechanic hadn't put back the tire kit, so I had to call AA or whatever they call that service."

"I'm sorry, Samantha," I say, half supportive and half irritated. "If I'd known, I'd have come and swept you away—"

"In your boat" she says humorlessly.

"I have magic powers," I reply on automatic. I don't do well when anger is directed at me, so for the moment I bury my instinct to strike back. "Are you on the road now? Are you okay?" I ask solicitously while working to relax the knot in my gut.

"I'm okay now. I've got my music, a bootlegged version of *American Beauty* when the band wasn't looking, and some new hot Cajun. I'm in good shape," she says, the cloud seeming to have passed. "So what are you doing with your beautiful body now? Give me the complete picture."

"I was fixing the boat, then reading—"

"Are you naked?"

"No, are you?"

"Not yet."

I feel the switch go on, my frustration and anger melting in the path of her explicitness. "When, then?"

"When I get off the Cape—I can't let loose on the Cape, too many memories under that bridge—but on the road with the warm wind I like to get comfy. At least partially."

I picture truckers and others enjoying the ride as she passes by: sunglasses, blonde hair, and little else. An odd twinge of jealousy slips in, but hey, if I'm going to be the benefactor of her sexy nature, I'd better be willing to tolerate its other manifestations. I have no idea if she did partially disrobe that warm day in August, and I don't care to ask. "And when are you coming to visit?" she asks. "Prescott isn't far, I promise you. There I keep *all* my tricks."

Our conversation ends soon after. While it leaves me aroused, I also feel whiplashed. She counted on me being present for her during her scary moment with the tire, but she seemingly couldn't accept a rational explanation for my being unavailable. She admonished me, but rewarded me too so I would not remain alienated by her. I am not going to be a fast study of Samantha, but she sure kicks up my curiosity and willingness to be a keen student.

Maybe, as my parent's generation had it, opposites attract. Yet can't those very same differences also contribute to disharmony, especially within the longer-term, repetitive scenarios of a partnership? What will happen, for example, when Samantha wants to go to endless numbers of parties and talk forever on the phone, and all I want to do after a long day is cuddle

Perhaps relationships are our best teaching vehicles, the fast track in our quest for personal growth.

up with her and a book? Will we have the equanimity then to embrace our differences, work with them, and allow them to shape us into more conscious beings?

One of my favorite cartoons from *The New Yorker* shows a couple engaged in a romantic dinner, complete with candelabra ablaze, wine glasses in hand, violinist hovering at the table, big smiles on both man and woman's faces, and body language bursting with heat. The thought bubble for the guy shows female body parts, scantily clad and accentuating the curves.

Meanwhile, the woman's thought bubble shows a guy dressed in work clothes, a house with a car out front, and a family: mommy, daddy, and four kids.

Plenty of heat at the dinner table—they probably could have lit the candles without a match. But how will her projections of what makes him attractive, and his notion of what is attractive in her, play out over time? Will he fall easily into the roles she dreams of for him? And how will his objectification of her unfold in the flush of daily life?

Ugh, as usual, I'm thinking about this too much. Isn't it good enough to just engage in the dance, and follow the music wherever it goes? Isn't the essence of romance, in life, about not knowing, and just being okay with that?

Perhaps relationships are our best teaching vehicles, the fast track in our quest for personal growth; or, our most efficient vehicle for connecting to the god within. All is good—even the pain. More cosmically, aren't we really all One anyway? Maybe there isn't even an *other* in the mix; it's just the universe playing both sides.

In All Her Glory

13
Three Guys in a Small Boat

Since landing in SNE, time has moved along quickly, with immersion into maintenance for *Kairos*, learning the nuances of sailing her (especially alone), connecting with friends, and spending time with, yes, Samantha. Overall, it feels like an unnaturally truncated summer and an October that has come way too soon.

Well into the fall Samantha continues to excite and annoy me. She invites me to her house in Prescott, just over the New Hampshire/Massachusetts border where she's been renting a one-story wood-frame structure facing William's pond. We plan the weekend, but she can't remember the dates we've agreed on. She is driven by impulse, one hundred percent.

Driving down Juniper Lane this crisp day, with windows open, I spot what must be her house. It lies along a wooded road with mostly summer houses dotted among the trees. Even without the benefit of a number on the mailbox, I know it is hers—I can see it breathe. Her energy is pouring out of it, even affecting the way the house occupies its place on the land. Nature conforms to her, not the other way around.

Samantha runs towards the rental car, her warm smile and blue eyes focused intently on me. I swallow hard, choking up with excitement and delight. At some point I become aware that her energy is sinking into me. I am hungry for it, as though I have been starved for a long time. She is warming me up, breaking apart some of the rock that has formed early on and remained over the years.

She helps me in with my bags and the groceries. No sooner do I have a chance to put the wine out and throw things in the fridge than she is all over me, kissing me and unbuttoning my clothes, then pulling me to the couch—that deep white couch, where we enter a new, fiery land. We drink lots of good wine and eat a bit of food, then somehow manage to sleep a few minutes before the morning sun starts creeping across the pond toward the trees. Peering out those picture windows in the cool morning light, I think to myself, *wouldn't it be good if we ended it right here? Don't even wake her up, Ed. Just slip away and let it be just a sexy dream.*

As we make breakfast of eggs scrambled easy with home-made English muffins, goat cheese, and roasted peppers, we talk of music, local politics, and yoga. She even has a present for me: my very own copy of the classic Buddhist text *I Am That*, the spiritual classic by Sri Nisargadatta. She may look like a Playboy bunny—and often acts like one—but underneath she has depth to burn, when she lets me find it. To each subject Samantha brings her own twist of insight and amusing anecdote. But when I ask her to personalize one of her stories in a way that might tell me more about her, she veers off quickly.

"Tell me, Samantha," I say in a light, interested way, "what don't I know about you that I should?"

"What you see is what you get. No stories, only the present." She looks at me and nods, saying, "That's all that's real, right? The present."

In some ways she echoes my own thoughts, because the past doesn't necessarily predict the future, but the past is interesting, and opens up common denominators, or reveals a better understanding of the present. I don't care to hear graphic stories of past escapades, but I am curious about what's shaped this blistering ball of energy.

"Don't let your eggs get cold," she says, directing my eyes to the plate and away from her.

Besides avoidance, she seems to be always kicking the intensity up a notch. I'm beginning to wonder whether the two behaviors are connected.

It isn't stimulating enough for us to just swim across the beautiful lake across from her house while experiencing the refreshing flow of cool water on our bodies; she needs to do it topless. And she loves making it a secret until, swimming along; she pulls me close to her, caresses me, and wants to have sex in the water right then and there. Rather than hold those feelings, I say, "Race you to the dock" to which she responds by turning into a silvery fish, propelled by some kind of force that doesn't flow through me. Beautiful to watch, her movements are smooth and powerful as she pulls herself through the water, passes me, and reaches the dock triumphant. I am close behind and not trying very hard, but she takes enormous pleasure in this little victory.

Our nights out usually drip with excitement. There is always some skin to be revealed, and a very provocative undergarment to display. She revels in turning me on, and I, of course, cooperate. There is nothing predictable or tame about this woman. She loves playing the flamboyant seductress, and I take it in fully as our drama deepens.

All this is fine for the times I want to be titillated, but what about the rest of our lives, the other 95 percent? I am old enough to know that the bedroom isn't the only room in the house, even if my body argues otherwise at times. Will her volatile, aggressive energy ever transform itself into something more cuddly?

"You love it when I come after you," she insists. "You're just upset by my initiative. You can't stand being with a woman with as much power as you."

"I don't think that's it at all—it's a matter of balance. I love making love, but—"

"You're being coy and hypocritical." She turns towards me in the kitchen, and for a moment I think she'll attack me.

"I'm only saying, this fire can't last—"

"You can't keep it up. It's too hot for you."

"No—"

"Then what, damn it?"

"Play nice. Talk to me. It doesn't have to be wildness and sex 24/7. I don't believe I'm saying this; most guys would love—"

"You're right, most guys would. So what's your problem?"

Round and round we go, and then when I'm alone I curse myself for pushing her away. All too often displeasure turns to dislike, and then into fights. Holding the conflicting energies of attraction and anger wears on me. I will need time and distance to put the pieces together. As the calendar ticks off more days, I grow increasingly thankful for the potential—albeit temporary—relief of a sail south.

Turning trees and dropping temperatures signal the crucial question: whether to sail or not. Heading toward warmer weather for the winter has, of course, been a foregone conclusion. After all, I can't sail in New England during the winter, so heading back to Florida is my only option. Or is it?

Sometime during September, under the influence of Samantha and what has become an almost obsessive attraction to her, I begin to think of putting *Kairos* "on the hard" up north for the winter, splitting my time partly in the northeast with Samantha, and partly at the Cocoa Beach condo. Talk about hormonal interference—and at my age. Isn't living on *Kairos* year round a key component of my journey? Am I thinking with a part of my anatomy that wasn't designed for thinking?

By the second week in October most "snow-boaters" have already headed south, yet I am still moored in ambivalence. If I decide to go for it, there will be time-consuming issues of selecting crew, planning the route, and finding a good weather window supportive of a safe sail. But I am beginning to run out of time. Unable to commit, I price out keeping *Kairos* up north for the winter, inside and well-protected. At roughly $18,000, the pressure to make a decision only increases.

Colder weather, which has already begun to set in adds to this growing sense of urgency. Mid-October 2009 is chillier than usual, with temperatures ranging from average lows of thirty-five degrees at night to daytime highs of barely fifty. It is now or never as the decision breakpoint creeps closer every day. Intuitively I sense the need to stick to my original plan for both spiritual and monetary reasons, but clarity of direction seems to be taking its time showing up.

Then, like a thunderbolt, I awake one day in mid-October to the imperative of leaving—now. The ambiguity is gone, phew. But the task before me is momentous. So, around Columbus Day I kick into planning mode with all the intensity of a brewing storm.

Kairos needs one final tweak to calibrate her radar system, and I need to line up at least two sailors. Partly due to the lack of available crew, and partly wanting to minimize the risks with me as a first-time captain, I begin thinking of the trip in three segments: New England to Norfolk, Virginia, staying "outside" the entire way; Norfolk to Cape Fear, North Carolina, staying inside by taking the Intracoastal Waterway; and then back out into the Atlantic for the final sail down to Florida.

This strategy will leave me in protected waters for the middle third, and keep me relatively close to shore (within seventy-five miles) for the other two legs. Overall, this is a safer plan than staying outside the entire way as we did on the trip north. It will also limit my having to navigate around the northerly flow of the Gulf Stream and feared Cape Hatteras. Plus, I will have the option of changing out crews for the different segments if necessary, since there is an airport close to each departure point. But for now, my focus is on the first leg: getting out of New England before it gets too cold and stormy to do so.

With this plan, my task of identifying an initial team is minimized, since the crew need only commit to the segment from New England to Norfolk. Including return transportation, this will be a four to five day commitment. My first break comes when a good friend and former business partner tells me he's willing to sign up. Jon and I have worked together for the past twenty-five years in one capacity or another, and we have also enjoyed a bit of recreational sailing during that time. He is the smartest guy I've ever met, and someone who gets the maximum response for the least amount of effort from everything he touches. Plus he has the best-tamed ego I have ever had the pleasure of *not* meeting.

Finding a compatible sailing partner isn't as complicated as finding a life partner, but there are similarities. Fortunately Jon and I know each other well, and we have learned to appreciate the complementary nature of our differences. Our prior experience had shown that we could flow together seamlessly, making decisions and executing tasks with mutual respect for one another.

That leaves one more spot to fill. While Jon and I have plenty of sailing experience, we both lack real hands-on mechanical knowledge. It only takes me a few seconds to flash on my brother Tom, who at first blush possesses all the right skills. He has little sailing experience but is a heck of a good mechanic, and he retired in June.

It's been years since I've spent an extended period of time with Tom. This could be an excellent opportunity to reconnect with one of my three siblings. As a bonus, I sense that he and Jon will enjoy each other. So I put a full-court press on him to join the Ed and Jon show. To my surprise, he quickly agrees. And with that I have a crew for the first leg—or so I think.

Before departing there are the usual last-minute errands, like provisioning *Kairos* with food and other critical supplies for the roughly 1200 nautical mile return trip to central Florida. And there are also, regretfully, some goodbyes to make, including the big one—Samantha.

This leave-taking is at one level getting easier, and at another pretty wearing. Repetition helps to clear the path and make it more recognizable, but I am not looking for clarity—I want connection. Over the three-month stay in SNE, I reconnected with familiarity—the people and places that fill me with friendship and beauty. And even something new and intriguing with the start of a possible long-term love affair. But now it is goodbye again to what I've become accustomed to, knowing little more than the vessel I will be traveling in, and what a compass bearing can show me.

It feels good that I am staying the course, continuing to follow my spirit wherever it wants to go. But my feelings' center—that soft pulsing heart in the middle of my chest—flirts instead with buying a small cottage on beautiful Martha's Vineyard and staying the winter. I do make vague arrangements for Samantha to join me for one of the legs south, and to exchange visits with her during the winter. But for now, I am sailing off into the emptiness with my future unknown.

Meanwhile, the goodbye embrace with Samantha is a mixed bag. I want more of her, and I've also had quite enough of her. *Changing the scene will add perspective,* I think to myself. *Maybe our connection just needs more time before the rough edges are smoothed out?*

"So then, I'll see you," I say as she steps off of *Kairos* for the last time. "Will you miss me?" I ask with more vulnerability than I intend.

"I'll miss *our* boat—*Kairos* is my buddy—but you're okay too." She sends me a dazzling smile. "Stay safe," she says. And as her words strike my ears, I realize it is the first really tender thing she's said to me in two and a half months, as though she cared for me, and not what I represented to her.

Tom, Jon, and I leave from West Falmouth on Cape Cod one day after final calibrations to the navigational system. We head directly for Block Island, a trip of roughly sixty miles, pointing initially west down Vineyard Sound and then continuing across open ocean to the small island itself. Block Island, approximately twelve miles east-northeast of the eastern tip of Long Island, NY, is a favorite departure point for many sailors heading south due to its location on the western edge of New England waters. From that point there's a clear shot at Norfolk, Cape Hatteras, or other strategic points.

But now it is goodbye again to what I've become accustomed to, knowing little more than the vessel I will be traveling in, and what a compass bearing can show me.

Most of the day has been sparkling clear with a cooperating wind, a beautiful first day for our shakedown cruise. I love being in the presence of both mates, and my hunch on the compatibility of Jon and Tom seems to be right on.

We arrive at Block Island harbor just as dark clouds are moving in. Perfect. Sailors watch for a low frontal system to pass through and then ride the clearing wind behind it, which is almost always out of the northwest. Our trip to Norfolk will have us heading southwest, creating what sailors call a beam reach, or what occurs when the wind is almost directly perpendicular to the boat, its maximum point of stability and speed.

Before settling in for dinner, we take the dinghy to shore. To my surprise, the normally bustling island is almost completely shut down for the winter. Even access to diesel fuel—an absolute necessity before leaving—requires special permission to unlock the pumps.

With internet access, we check the latest weather reports on our planned Atlantic route. Jon—a brilliant technology guru—introduces us to software that shows graphically the predicted wind direction, speed, and moisture conditions five days out in ongoing three-hour segments. I usually don't get excited about these kinds of things, but this software is the ultimate in cool, and just what is needed.

Initially we are elated, since the new tool confirms prior reports that the oncoming storm will be moving through overnight. But then we see the next storm, one that hasn't been previously forecast. This powerful mass of wind and moisture is estimated to be approximately 180 miles southwest of Block Island in two days—exactly where I estimate we will be with a morning departure. The prediction is for a mean and nasty disturbance—forty-plus mph winds and heavy rainfall. The color software graphics make it all the more foreboding with an intense purple designating the storm center. I might be anxious to leave New England behind, but knowingly sailing into that mess would be downright crazy. Even irresponsible.

Hungry and tired, we resolve to enjoy the evening anyway. I prepare a sumptuous Northern Italian dinner, which we lubricate with generous amounts of wine, washing down the food and our feelings of disappointment. How often do three guys get to feel really close and enjoy a serious adventure together? None of us want to let go of that sense of camaraderie.

We rise early the next morning to recheck the updated computer simulations, which now look at least as unfavorable as the evening before. What to do? One option is to wait out the next storm, but that would mean a delay of two or three days. And unfortunately neither Jon nor Tom has that kind of flexibility in their schedules. Finally we accept the only reasonable alternative: halt progress and take the ferry back to the mainland, leaving *Kairos* moored to face the storm alone. Tom and Jon return to their homes, and I am out of a crew, just like that.

Father and Son

14
Slapped by the Ocean

Back on the mainland, I rent a car and check into the Comfort Inn (an oxymoron if I ever heard one, and certainly under these conditions). Ugh, what a predicament. I am sequestered in a chilly motel room while *Kairos* is out on the mooring at Block Island. Meanwhile, I have no idea of how, or if, I can get out of SNE. It all feels as if I'm trapped in a film noir movie.

But it's not in my nature to stay down for long. Noticing the phone, I begin putting it to good use. Initially I hadn't contacted Evan about coming on the trip since he is in session at NYU. Now, however, I'm getting desperate. Despite the possibility of being viewed as an irresponsible dad, I put through the call. No surprise—he is eager to go and will check his schedule to see if joining me just after storm number two passes through is a possibility.

"Sure Dad, I can make it work with minimal academic damage."

I ask no questions.

Evan and I can most likely handle the three-day trip to Norfolk on our own, and I'm tempted to do so just to move things along. However, I have already skated along the edge of parental irresponsibility by tempting him away from his studies.

Adding carelessness to my captain's résumé isn't looking like an attractive option.

As chance would have it, I'd run into a chap named Jonah when Jon, Tom, and I were still on Block Island. There Jonah runs a small charter fishing business during the summer, but as the season draws to an end, he is looking for any kind of work he can find. I took his phone number just in case, and now I'm feeling thankful I did. A quick call from the motel confirms he is available for the sail south, and is happy for the opportunity.

Jonah is an avid surfer, and looks it. He catches the eye of every female he passes—regardless of age—with his abundant crop of blonde highlighted hair that always seems perfectly tousled, plus just enough muscle peeking out of his stretched-tight t-shirts to say he can get the job done. His look is part sweetness and part aloofness, which I learn later through observation is fatally attractive to the opposite sex. Despite his biblical name and head-turning good looks, during our chance encounter, and on the phone, he seems easygoing and eager to please.

With crew confirmed, I move into a friend's house in nearby Providence for an overnight of friendly conversation and a home-cooked meal. Life is improving quickly. Evan comes up by train the next day from New York City, and we have our navigation strategy meeting over dinner. Very early the next morning, both of us take the ferry out to Block Island, meet our new crewmate Jonah, and steam out of the harbor by midmorning.

We head directly southwest toward Norfolk with the predicted northwest breeze cooperating on our beam. As a bonus, there is a stunning view to starboard of the eastern tip of Long Island: Montauk Point and its famed lighthouse. I'd spent many vacations there as a kid, which now adds a bit of sweet nostalgia to the mix of emotions.

The latest computer-generated reports, checked just before departure, show a favorable wind scenario continuing from the northwest, while diminishing in strength over the next few days. Then I make my big mistake: I believe them.

Day one materializes as predicted, but by day two, approximately 150 nautical miles from Block Island, the wind begins to swing around first to the west and then—worse—to the southwest. Plus, the wind strength keeps increasing rather than decreasing. That leaves us with three options:

1) Maintain our southwest course toward Norfolk, but under engine power and into strong oncoming wind and surf.

2) Continue sailing, but on an altered course more southeast than southwest, which would push us further out to sea.

3) Tack back toward New York City and lose considerable ground.

Right, I think, *no good options*. After much deliberation and considerable hesitation, Evan and I choose option # 2.

As the afternoon hours tick by and the approaching late-October darkness looms, I find myself growing increasingly apprehensive. The most recent forecast for the following day is favorable, calling for the wind direction to resettle northwest, and diminishing in strength. But what if that doesn't happen? By daylight we will be further out to sea and off our direct southwest course by as much as fifty miles—a much longer way back to safety if we need it. Bouncing around the cabin, the stakes seem high, and I'm finding it hard to hide my nervousness.

Evan sometimes knows me better than I do. Noticing me obsessing while catching a bite of dinner he immediately moves closer, puts his arm around my shoulder, and says, "Dad, relax, *I've* got it under control. The options have been considered, and for now we've made the best available choice. What I want you to do is finish your dinner and get some rest. Your watch will be here in no time."

This is surely a milestone moment, I think, *not just for the trip, but more broadly, and more poignantly, for our relationship.* Here the first mate is taking charge as the captain, and the son is assuming his first steps in capturing the mantle of responsibility from the father. Whoa, am I ready for this?

Just shy of twenty-one, Evan has been sailing with me since he was eleven weeks old—well, he *was* on the boat. First, family trips including his mom, and then mostly just the two of us. Sailing was a constant in our lives, an activity around which we developed a close bond. I've always considered myself fortunate to have a son who enjoys something so dear to my heart.

Over the years we experienced many challenges that required our full and coordinated attention. Learning to depend on each other, our trust grew as our mutual skills deepened. I have often commented to friends that there aren't many people I would hand the wheel to in a crisis. Evan is at the top of a very short list.

Yet, in all cases, I have been the captain and he the mate. I've had both the control and the ultimate responsibility. There wasn't any question who was in charge, or who was learning from whom. Then, a few years ago, a few subtle changes began to emerge. I was getting older, which meant more forgetful, less quick at navigational strategy, and certainly less daring. At the same time, Evan was growing into a very mature, super-quick decision maker with plenty of moxie. When discussing decisions he would often be ahead of me on the logic curve. What really took me by surprise, however, was his growing and very sweet concern for my safety.

One day, several years ago, we had been on the water since early morning when the winds were calm and didn't call for lifejackets. By late afternoon though, conditions had changed, with us sailing fully reefed and into a very brisk breeze. At one point Evan said to me gently, "Dad, do you think you should put on your lifejacket?" I knew at that moment that the current of our sailing relationship had changed direction, and it was only a matter of time before the roles reversed.

Back to our trip down to Norfolk, I take Evan's advice and go to bed, awaking from a deep sleep in time to relieve Jonah at three in the morning. Typically, when changing shifts, the person coming on duty is briefed by the person going off. And I am still the captain, at least in title. Entering the cockpit, it is obvious that the wind direction has already shifted back to the west, and that the sails and direction of the boat have been adjusted to give us a more favorable tack. I knew Jonah hadn't executed the changes without direction—it must be Evan.

Then, almost immediately, Jonah says to me, respectfully, "Wow, Evan sure knows how to sail. We're heading right back where we want to be, and thankfully much closer to shore."

"Yeah," I say, "he sure does," which further confirms that the incident earlier last evening is but the first of more to come. By the end of my shift three hours later, the wind has already begun to decrease as predicted. So we turn directly into the moderating surf, start the engine, and head directly for Norfolk at full speed.

Day three is a welcome respite from the intensity of the first two days. The wind gradually loses its punch, the seas follow suit, and the sky grows clear, allowing us to just hang out and relax. Already I can feel the warmer air. We have sailed out of late fall and back into summer in just two days. New England and its impending winter are now clearly behind us.

Based on current speed, our calculations show us getting to the heavily trafficked northern Chesapeake Bay entrance by midnight. We slow *Kairos* down to three and a half knots, which puts us on track for an early morning arrival when visibility will be better. Sure enough, by daylight of the following morning, we begin to see the impressive span of the Chesapeake Bay Bridge (which is more like a very long jetty connecting Newport News on the north to Norfolk on the south). There before us is the northern "bite" where the Bridge takes a nosedive underwater to become a tunnel, thus allowing nautical traffic to pass above.

From the water it is a most impressive sight, made even more so that morning by a spectacular ocean sunrise.

Evan has just arrived in the cockpit to relieve me for his 6 a.m. shift. The two of us stand together in reverential silence, observing the increasingly sunlit bridge ahead of us, and the beautiful fiery red globe behind us as it lifts first up, then above, the horizon. It is one of those rare moments when roles dissolve and personalities merge. Of no concern to either of us is who claims captain and who claims mate, or even who is father and who is son. All that matters is our being here together. Since Evan's birth, I have always felt that fathering this amazing boy is a large part of my work on earth. Now, standing together in the awe of exquisite beauty and closeness, I feel the rightness, and completeness, of that divine assignment.

Of no concern to either of us is who claims captain and who claims mate, or even who is father and who is son. All that matters is our being there together.

Our approach to the entrance has us staying out of the traffic lane. Getting closer, we see an imposing string of commercial freighters, many of them at least twenty times our length, lined up and ready to enter the Bay. Evan and I decide to navigate this one together, especially when we begin to hear the "Naval speak" over the radio: "This is warship number thirty-seven engaged in military maneuvers. All craft are advised to stay away or face the possibility of force."

The word *force* clearly catches my attention. Evan utters a marginally respectful, "Holy shit." This is Norfolk, home to the second largest naval flotilla in America. We aren't going to argue with any of them, either the warships or the freighters. So we very carefully negotiate the entrance, and then the channels leading us down the Bay to our stopping point for the night, a spiffy marina right at the entrance to the famed Intracoastal Waterway.

Due to the unpredicted wind shifts, the trip has taken longer than predicted, which makes Evan anxious to get back to New York City for his classes. I am pleased to be safe and tied to a dock, which we pull into at a little past noon. Jonah and I fill up with fuel while Evan makes a flight reservation online. Within minutes, he is packed and in a taxi speeding toward the Norfolk airport to catch his mid-afternoon flight. I feel relieved about our arrival and the completion of this phase south but, as always, I am sad to see Evan leave. Will I ever get used to these alternating periods of connection and separation?

The Intracoastal

15
Takin' It Easy

After cleaning *Kairos* from the trip (somehow since the age of two Evan has always managed to escape this part), I sit on the dock feeling disoriented, unsure of the next step, and a little fearful of that looming grey edge of loneliness. Over the past few weeks my focus has been exclusively on getting out of New England. With that now behind me, the path forward is anything but clear.

Immediately to my right is a huge shopping center replete with neon everything and loud music oozing out the doors. To my left is the entrance to the Intracoastal heading south. I have no appetite for the former, and I am apprehensive of the latter. Plus I'm exhausted from the trip and missing both Evan and Samantha. *What about the status of my remaining crew member Jonah?* I wonder. *Will he leave, or stick it out to the end?* It all feels surreal, which has me wondering what I'm doing here in the first place.

In the midst of confusion, I call Samantha. Unfortunately it is one of those all-too-frequent times when her voice is audible, but there is no presence. We speak for only a few minutes. It feels like talking to an inanimate object, with canned questions and replies. *Why can't she just show up?* I wonder in frustration. *Is that so hard?*

I long for a time when she calls *me* for support, and allows *me* to be the hero. Or when she senses I need a comforting hand and extends her own. Desire, yes—intimacy and caring…those aren't qualities I've seen from this woman, at least not yet.

Hanging up, I gather my strength to begin weighing the sailing options. I'll need information. In my rush to get out of New England, I chose to defer doing research for the trip south of Norfolk. Fortunately, this place is filled with yachters either about to enter the Intracoastal or relaxing after having just finished the northward passage. Basically, all the local knowledge I'll need, just waiting in their boats.

Within an hour I have the scoop on how to navigate the often-narrow channel with low water on both sides. Plus, I learn the schedules for frequent drawbridges and occasional water-leveling locks, along with the best places to stop for the night. Yet, even with this new stash of information, my concern remains high. I am hesitant to jump into this inland waterway without having experienced its unfamiliar challenges firsthand. It seems very complicated, just waiting for a novice like me to falter. And I'm in desperate need of rest.

But first, it is time to talk to Jonah and see what he is thinking. One thing is certain: if I decide to continue south on the Intracoastal, I can't do it alone.

I already feel simpatico with Jonah. It must be partly due to the fact that we were born on the same day (June 26), and thus carry the same cosmic energetic imprint of Cancer the Crab (or the more flattering label of Moonchild). His personality is delightfully unassuming (so much for the similarity). And we seem to view much of life through the same lens.

On the trip down, Jonah had been the perfect complement for Evan and me. At thirty-three he is able to understand a bit of both ends of the forty-two-year age spectrum, while offering his own middle position. He is experienced in fishing, surfing, and, of course, women, which always makes for rich conversations.

While he comes with little hands-on sailing experience, Jonah is at home on the ocean, super strong, and a fast, eager, learner. I couldn't have written a more apt job description for our second mate, who is now about to (hopefully) become my first mate.

Jonah notices me up ahead on the dock and leans forward. We nod at each other, and he says, accompanied with a wry smile, "So, do you think we should talk, captain?"

"Sure," I say, finding a comfortable spot to sit. "I was just going to see what you were up to. Ya know, I'm in a bit of a quandary. I can see staying in Norfolk a few days to recuperate or…head on down the waterway without delay. Any thoughts?"

"I'm good either way," he says. "Just another wave for this surfer boy."

Hum, I think, *not a bad metaphor for melting away some of those attachments.* Maybe I should abandon sailing and take up surfing. Or, more appropriately, maybe I should study Jonah more carefully, especially the way he meets the waves of life without prior expectations.

Pulling my attention back toward Jonah, I nod and say, "Good, so you're able to stay either way?"

"I'm in—it's all good."

I can't help but notice his bright blue eyes and easy smile. I envy that ability of his to be fully present and wonder for a moment if he's available as a tutor for someone I know up north.

After a bit more processing and a brief trip to a nearby grocery store for provisions, we decide to get a good night's sleep and see how life looks in the morning. Drifting off into dreamland that evening, I'm convinced we have at least another day in Norfolk before moving on.

But life looks different this morning, as it often does. I feel surprisingly rested and alert. It immediately occurs to me that it's still early enough to make the drawbridge before rush hour. So, in an instant, my body kicks into gear as I let out a loud shout to Jonah, who is still asleep, "Okay Jonah, we're heading out, now." I turn the key and the engine roars to life. Jonah stumbles through the main hatch from below as we throw off the dock lines, then pass right through the downtown drawbridge with only a minute to spare.

Leaving Norfolk in our wake, we pass the remaining and very imposing stock of naval hardware—ship after ship after large ship, most of them battle-ready with impressive firepower. A child of the late forties/early fifties, just as General Eisenhower was transitioning to President Eisenhower, I can't help but reflect on his concern for the dangers of an over-inflated military-industrial complex. Sure looks to me today like no one heard him, much less heeded his warning. I also find myself reflecting on the modern-day equivalent, Secretary of Defense Robert M. Gates, who likes to point out when making the responsible (in my view) argument for a more streamlined force, that our naval battle fleet is larger than the next thirteen navies combined, eleven of which belong to allies and partners.

... maybe I should study Jonah more carefully, especially the way he meets the waves of life without prior expectations.

My mind is busy calculating the number of baseball fields, concert halls, hospitals, schools, and museums that can be built for the cost of even one of these hunks of steel whose shadows we are passing through.

Surprisingly, day one on the Intracoastal is a hoot, with lots of new and interesting experiences. As we proceed south on our journey down the Intracoastal, it all feels damn good. Which proves to me, once again, that one second of whole-body wisdom is worth a few days of rational agonizing. The lessons seem endless, and well choreographed. Whoever thought up this life curriculum sure had a healthy appetite for growth, and a robust sense of humor.

Timing the drawbridge passages and negotiating the water-leveling locks falls into place without much trouble. Up to this point I've been thinking of the Intracoastal route as a poor cousin to an ocean passage, something one did as a last resort, and only to avoid rough weather on the outside. But as we pass interesting towns, and even more interesting natural attractions such as bays, rivers, uninhabited islands, and abundant wildlife, I begin to change my mind.

The "ditch" portions (human-made waterway connectors) are particularly appealing, since they bring the wildlife—especially a great number and variety of birds—within a few feet of the boat. The immediacy of the experience is breathtaking. It often feels like I can reach out and touch these beautiful beings. They love flying low and directly overhead, seemingly curious about the interlopers

... one second of whole-body wisdom is worth a few days of rational agonizing.

passing through their wetlands at a much slower pace, and with far less grace.

Jonah and I are headed toward Beaufort, North Carolina, approximately 180 miles down the Waterway. It is one of the East Coast's premier yachting centers, and the same harbor Evan, Brett and I stayed at for repairs on the sail north just four months ago. At six knots, that means either three rather aggressive, or four shorter, days.

I am in no rush, but there is the question of timing for Samantha. Before leaving Rhode Island we planned for her to join the trip at some point, and Beaufort now seems like the best alternative. There is an airport nearby, which will facilitate a one-week exchange of first-mates.

Jonah and I spend the initial night out of Norfolk in Coinjock, North Carolina. It is conveniently located at mile 50 on the Intracoastal, making it the stopover of choice for most passage-makers. The literal definition of Coinjock is "Land of the Mulberries." This adds to our curiosity since, according to the locals, there are no mulberries to be found.

As we steam into town, I notice the fancy Coinjock Marina and Restaurant on the east side, while on the west hails the funkier Midway Marina and its restaurant, affectionately named Crabbies. *Kind of cute*, I think, as we take the last available dock slip right in front of the restaurant. It isn't until I pay for the night and tie off the lines that someone says, "The band at Crabbies is wild. You'll love it—plays right outside there, literally fifty feet from you all." So much for the hoped-for peaceful, quiet evening in this quaint town without mulberries.

A night out at Crabbies seems mildly attractive. I have plenty of fresh food on board that needs to be eaten, and we can always hear the band for free just a few feet away. But we do need something to drink as a celebration after our first day on the Waterway. Jonah sniffs out a source for beer and offers to fetch some if the captain pays for it. Lickety-split he arrives back with a six-pack of Bud Light for himself, and two imported nut-brown ales for me. *Part of a surfer's resume?* I wonder.

Even back then they knew that suffering came from an over-identification with our own thoughts.

We finish dinner as the dreaded band begins to tune. Oh what I would give for some Beethoven string quartets at this moment. Jonah finishes his six-pack and takes off to Crabbies bar around back while I brace myself for the evening's entertainment.

I'm into beer number two when the band cranks it up. Much to my surprise, there in the cockpit of *Kairos* under the clear North Carolina sky, I begin to enjoy the music. While the quality is pure downtown Coinjock, their repertoire is surprisingly what I need at the moment: the classics of the sixties and seventies. The energy flows in and out of me, stimulating and soothing at the same time. Oh my, I'm actually having a good time in spite of myself.

Halfway through the second set, the band pulls out the big one, the tune that for me captures that entire era: "Take it Easy" by the Eagles. I haven't heard it in years, and I don't remember most of the words, but on this replay the classic song appears both deeply reflective and richly prophetic. The directness of the words on this balmy late-October night seem almost make believe as I take them in and tap my foot instinctively to the delightful rhythms.

There sure is a lot of wisdom packed into that one tune, I think. If only I'd played by the song's script for the last forty years, I wouldn't be having so much difficulty now with this transition. Even back then they knew that suffering came from an over-identification with our own thoughts, or from the folly of thinking that we can understand with our minds alone anything really worth understanding. And the one bit of wisdom I completely missed, and have paid for dearly over the years: romantic love does not solve all. My hard-earned school-of-life lesson is that God is inside, and most attempts to find her outside—especially through someone else—end in more suffering.

Somewhere in the mix of that evening's events, I meet the couple on the boat next to us. They are very generous in pointing out both the dangers and the opportunities between Coinjock and Beaufort, all of which turn out to be accurate and very helpful in the days ahead. But I am baffled by their partnership. He is a mild-mannered, lethargic older guy,

> *... God is inside, and most attempts to find her outside—especially through someone else—end in more suffering.*

while she has enough youthful vigor to light up the marina. She certainly turns on my lights. *More evidence concerning the mystery of relationships,* I muse. Speaking of relationships, it is now only a few days until reuniting with Samantha, the queen of light-lighters, and the most complex woman I've ever experienced.

Finally giving in to sleep, my mind wanders to an imaginary bar where Jonah holds court for at least a dozen attractive women. In a moment of bittersweet nostalgia, my vivid fantasy reminds me that my time for doing things like that is fading (or has it already?).

I'm not sure when Jonah makes it back to *Kairos,* and I really don't want to know, but we are up early the next day and ready to face the challenges ahead. Winds are predicted to be turbulent this afternoon, so we have to be on our way. Besides, Samantha's scheduled arrival in Beaufort is now only three days away.

All is well until we hit Albemarle Sound a little after noon. At that point the large body of water is a good thirty miles wide and generally quite shallow. Add in a twenty-eight-knot wind, and uncomfortably choppy conditions prevail. Sailing through it would be no problem, but the wind is on our nose, which means we have to motor right into the messy, erratic surf. After two hours, Jonah and I decide to pack it in for the day, finding a little-known harbor at the southern end of the Sound: the Alligator River Marina.

As with Coinjock and the nonexistent mulberries, there are no alligators, but thankfully the entrance is easy. Once in, it is hardly noticeable that the wind is blowing hard out on the Sound. We are only about fifteen miles west of Kitty Hawk of the Wright Brothers fame, which roughly defines the center point of the Outer Banks, or just a few miles north of feared Cape Hatteras. We may have experienced some sailing discomfort today, but I don't want to even think about what it would have been like attempting to get around the Hatteras shoals in a twenty-eight-knot blow. Alligator Marina isn't elegant, and doesn't fully live up to its name, but it is safe, peaceful, and without a restaurant or band to keep us up late.

Day three is long but enjoyable, with the winds having backed down, and no large open bodies of water to traverse. Despite the rough weather yesterday, we did manage to clock thirty-five miles, putting Beaufort only 120 miles away, or within two day's reach. I've now experienced my fill of marinas, which has me itching for a calm anchorage surrounded by a beautifully wooded landscape. And that is precisely what we find at the end of the quiet Pungo River.

I haven't been in contact with Samantha since Norfolk, so just before dinner I send her a text and set up a phone appointment for an hour later. She seems eager.

Not surprisingly, though, all through dinner I feel edgy and vulnerable about the upcoming connection. Even when we plan a call, Samantha is often highly distracted, with talk of intimacy the farthest thing from her mind. Why am I the one always looking for tenderness?

Stepping out to the cockpit for privacy, I finally reach her, but our cell phone connection is tenuous. "Hello, Samantha—Samantha, are you—oh, hi, can you hear me?"

"Is that you, Ed?"

"Yes, I'm calling from Pungo River." I feel like I'm shouting.

"Mango River?

"As sweet a place as a mango but no, Pungo—you can look it up on a map for fun."

"Why would I do that?" she asks, perplexed. "It's your idea to go tooling around on your boat."

This is not off to a good start. "How are you, whatcha been up to?"

"Nothing, just the regular stuff." She pauses, and I think she is going to add something but she doesn't. I hear papers rustling in the background, even a clanging pot or two.

"Samantha, did I catch you at a bad time?" I try to say calmly.

"No…the Internet's acting up and I'm trying to find something to eat, that's all—a recipe for something…vegetarian goulash. I had goulash at a friend's house and wanted to make it for myself."

"I thought we had a phone appointment?" I say with increasing frustration. "You knew from my text that I was going to call now, didn't you?"

"Well, I kinda lost track of the time. Can't you just loosen up a bit?"

Her distraction sends blood rushing to my face. I blurt out, "Christ, Samantha, can you put the damn internet away and the pots too while we talk for a moment? We haven't spoken in days, and I've just come in from a long day on the water after a rough storm yesterday. Plus it would be really good to connect."

"Well mister sailor boy, I'm so sorry I'm not ready to drop everything the moment you call. I have a life too, and while I'm not being blown around by the sea, I do have things to do."

"I think I'll call you later," I say and start to hang up when suddenly the wind shifts in her.

"Okay, Ed—that was probably a little too abrupt of me," she says, now seeming a bit more present and pitched to engage. "I know you were trying to tell me what you've been up to—sorry I was in the middle of things. Perhaps I should have managed my time better. After all, we did set this time aside."

I realize that I've jumped up in the midst of the conversation, so I sit back down and tell her, "Yeah, well I think I got spooked a bit from the storm and being so near Cape Hatteras and all the tragic history associated with it, and—"

"Sounds like something to put in your log—do you keep a log by the way?"

I am getting tangled in her distancing lines. "Yes, sometimes. Depends."

"I miss your arms," she says. "Where are you when I need you? I'm opening the Zin you gave me and thinking of what I'd do to you if you were here."

I resist playing along. "I also called about your coming down. You know, the exact time and other details." I hear her pop the cork and rustle around with what sounds like snacks to accompany the wine.

"Good. Great. You can string me up—lash me to the mast."

"I don't want to do that," I say, riding the edge of my rising anger. "But I'd like it if we could have more tenderness in our life together. I'd like to feel your sweetness in addition to your desire."

She shoots back, "Stop acting like a needy child."

We carry on, but our phones are both dying, protecting us from doing any more damage. I sit in the cockpit with my heart pounding in my chest. She's stiffed me with another one of those calls and conversations that keep shifting planes and never meeting. She told me once, "I'm a lousy person to come to with boo-boos." I guess my wanting to connect in a soft, comforting way is destined to fail. She clearly has a grip on me—most others would have pried her fingers from their body and walked away, but I'm not ready to do that yet.

We end another phone conversation at a stalemate, both feeling like we didn't get what we wanted. Maybe each of us is waiting for the right time and excuse to pull the plug for our own reasons.

Those phone bars indicating signal do reappear a few times over the rest of the evening, but I decide to leave us where we are.

That night, while lying in bed half asleep, I muse on the nature of our astrological imprints. I am a soft, watery crab, while Samantha is on the cusp of Aires and Taurus—half ram, half bull. *Not a bad thumbnail summary of our innate differences and the ensuing conflict they often bring*, I think. Maybe this obvious imbalance of personalities, and the implied inversion of masculine and feminine, suggests I should end it now before I get burned beyond recognition, but a voice deep inside clearly says, *Keep going, don't quit yet. Give it more time. There is something to learn here.*

Acting contrary to mounting evidence, and lured on by the prospect of a loving sailing partner, I keep hoping we can work things out. It is this image, this picture of partnership in my mind that keeps me going. I have somehow convinced myself that Samantha, or someone like her, is what will make it all okay, what will make me happy and buffer me from my loneliness. But the price I'm paying is getting too high. My mother was right—I hate being alone, so I keep sticking Samantha back in the cockpit. Maybe I'll find someone who can cook me goulash, and that will be enough. Throw in laundry, and we've got a deal.

Day four is pleasantly uneventful as Jonah and I meander down the Pamlico River, Goose Creek, Bay River, Neuse River, Adams Creek, and then finally on into Beaufort in time for a late celebratory dinner. These varied and multihued bodies of water are part of what make our trip down the Atlantic Intracoastal route so interesting.

Despite my wish to celebrate the culmination of this leg of the trip, dinner at the marina restaurant is muted. I'm sure Jonah picks up on my nervousness about Samantha's impending arrival, but out of respect for the captain he keeps his observations to himself. Meanwhile I'm running an internal dialogue. *Would the high maintenance required to support this union distract me, even jeopardize my ability to captain* Kairos? *More importantly, would I later view Samantha as a liability in keeping the good ship Ed afloat and sailing forward?*

Looking Toward Heaven

16

Calm Waters
or Self-Deception?

With Samantha's arrival imminent, and Jonah's departure soon upon me, a sense of dread sets in. The odd association of Cold War spies being exchanged comes to mind, only I'm not sure if I want this trade to go through.

The plan is for Samantha and me to advance *Kairos* from Beaufort to Bald Head Island, North Carolina, approximately 110 miles due south. Fortunately, Jonah needs this week to complete the move out of his Block Island summer apartment, and Samantha is able to take the same week off from her work at a local art gallery.

I am well aware of the denial of feelings surrounding the last phone call with Samantha, but I'm missing her, and want to connect with some of that uncut desire which she elicits in me. That said, I'm feeling cautious. I can temporarily override my need for tenderness, but only at a longer-term cost.

And I sense more complexity. There just has to be something other than what appears to be Samantha's need to hide her vulnerability under the guise of flashy sexuality and exaggerated independence. *What am I hiding? Isn't that the important question?* I think to myself. Isn't the over-focusing on heated sex a distraction for me, as well as for her? The need to guard whatever lurks beneath the surface couldn't be just one-sided. What is my role? And do I already know the answer, but need to conceal it from myself?

Feeling emotionally overloaded (plus I'm late), I rush to the airport with discussion tabled and fingers crossed.

I spot her in the walkway below. She moves like no one else. Maybe others would respond differently, but for me what she exudes is keyed to my core. Her animal lines and flamboyant grace thrill me. She throws her arms around my shoulders as we walk—hop really—holding hands to the baggage claim, and then to the car like a couple of teenagers. She smells of spearmint, potato chips, and her own distinct unwashed yet intoxicating scent. I am aroused, but I also feel my body tighten with resistance.

Her entrance feels energetically similar to that moment in August when she arrived on the ferry. She is highly assertive, with a clear sense of "I'm in the right place at the right time with the right guy." Even her body language screams, "Okay I'm here, so let's get this show on the road." I like her assertiveness. It excites me, and she knows it. But I am also put off by what I read as shallowness. Like a "pick" in basketball she is good at setting up deflections, *But can she put the ball in the basket?* I wonder. *Is she even interested in getting close to the basket?*

Once at the car, Samantha surprises me. Slamming the door she demands we get moving. "I'm hungry—get me to a restaurant FAST," she says, smiling but unmistakably insistent. Stamping her feet (playfully?) she calls out, "Pronto—I'm losing it."

Flash: *Oh my god. What is my mother doing here?* Of course she isn't really here, yet all of a sudden I can see her, hear her. Even feel her. She is young, powerful, and self-centered. She doesn't see me as I cry out for attention. My longing is deep and unattended to. Pressing my foot on the accelerator I feel unnerved by an immediate shot of anxiety.

My heart races. What's going on? Is Samantha reminding me of my mother? These two important women in my life do have a similar feel. Is that why I'm attracted to her, while I simultaneously resist her aggressive style? Do I desire her, and fear her, at the same time?

Once on *Kairos* Samantha slips into the cabin like it is hers, and I clamber after her only to hit my head going down the steps. Damn—even in the roughest of seas I've never hit my head. Yet chasing after her I see stars—painful ones. Feeling the bump on my head, I'm wondering if that universe I believe in has sent me another message. Over the next few days I'll see this as a warning shot across my thick skull, a clear signal that, for the moment, I choose to ignore.

We awake to a beautiful day with clear skies and moderate winds. Way back in Coinjock our neighbors recommended an unforgettable anchorage. "Cape Lookout," they said, "is only eight miles east of Beaufort Harbor and offers a lovely, romantic destination." The peace and tranquility of a quiet anchorage sounds like just what we need.

This most unusual geological formation appears on the nautical chart like a big hook, forming an inside circular body of water called Lookout Bight, approximately 1.5 miles in diameter and with average depths of a convenient twenty-five feet for anchoring. A narrow sand barrier creates the "hook," which is mostly protected national seashore. Despite a narrow entrance, once inside this safe haven affords yachters a much-protected place to relax and hang out, with views at a full 360 degrees.

By late morning we are on our way down the Beaufort harbor channel headed directly for Lookout Bight. Glancing over at Samantha with her smooth pearly skin and the wind in her sparkly hair, I wonder if those delightfully active hormones governing attraction ever decide they've had enough for one lifetime and just peacefully fade away. After all, at roughly the same age, we are well past the procreation hot zone. Our motivation is pure fun. Or is it? Maybe my suspicions are correct and there is a deeper, less tasteful reason for all this attention on carnal pleasure, like diversion from intimacy.

Once out of the harbor we choose the outside route, which offers a brief opportunity to test our combined skills on the open ocean. What I learn is to stay in protected waters unless conditions are calm. Samantha, who is almost as strong as Jonah, has lots of crew potential but almost no experience. I chuckle to myself—I should stay in protected waters *all* the time with Samantha.

By late afternoon we are sweetly nestled in, hanging just a few-hundred feet off the southern seashore. The wind has begun to blow, but we are mostly protected from it. And due to my favorite Northwest clearing wind, the visibility is impeccable. Among other treats, we have a direct view of the Cape Lookout Lighthouse a mile away, with its unusual black-and-white diamond pattern and persistent signaling light. A stellar example of late nineteenth-century lighthouses, it provides a constant amid the rise and fall of events on board.

Next day the wind is still blowing around eighteen to twenty knots, but it doesn't interfere with our plans to dinghy ashore and engage the beach. Both of us like to walk, and Samantha can keep up with any guy her age or younger. I do manage not to embarrass myself, although I am the one to finally say after four hours or so, somewhat sheepishly, "Do you think it's time to turn back?"

In her usual not so subtle way she replies, "Well sure, if you can't take it anymore." Her words sting. I'm tempted to react, but I bury the feeling instead—something I'm not particularly good at. Past experience tells me that it will resurface as resentment, or a retaliatory verbal blow, but I never know when.

The shoreline is nothing short of gorgeous, ringed with hopeful fishermen both on land and in their boats. We stop to speak with one couple who fishes here every October for a week, which gives them enough catch to fill up their freezer for a full year. Judging from their full buckets, they are well into next May's meal planning. Then back to *Kairos* for a beautifully composed dinner and a breathtaking sunset just west of the lighthouse.

Yet the romance for me is superficial. Rather than savoring the food and brilliant colors of the evening, Samantha keeps pushing the conversation and ambiance towards the events that she has already determined will unfold. I want to talk about North Carolina's coastal history and how lighthouses are late in coming to protect sailors from shifting sea beds, while she describes finding the right moment to show me something provocative she's found to wear. And while she in fact knows as much about the Civil War and wave mechanics from her general reading as I do, her focus lies elsewhere. That is, unless she wants to use her knowledge to best me, to win an argument, or to pull ahead somehow.

I want to wash the dishes before we go to bed; she wants to leave them piled in the sink. I want to check the weather reports for the next day; she takes that as an opportunity to run her hand up my shirt and tickle behind my ear. What guy wouldn't want that non-stop? Me. I love foreplay as much as the next guy, but without the richness that comes from connections of all types, the intended titillation feels shallow.

Watching Samantha move around the cabin my attention is drawn back to the way she appears to use her sexiness as a decoy. I find myself questioning again: what is she trying to hide? Perhaps more to the point, is there something about my own wounded nature that fears exposure? And if so, what is that? Perhaps Samantha's real purpose in this dance is to act like a mirror, reflecting back to me a more exaggerated version of myself. Is that what really scares me about her?

This short bout of self-reflection melts away quickly as we fly right back into active bouts of wild tiger sex. Yet despite the excitement and the idyllic location, I'm not able to relax. Among other indicators, my sleep is fitful, which has me worried. I need my strength to perform life-critical duties as the captain of this ship, especially with a novice crew member on board. Plus, the upcoming ocean leg with Jonah will likely challenge my stamina to the max. I clearly need to find a way to rejuvenate during this week. Samantha, on the other hand, has no such need, remaining as intense and demanding as ever.

I long for some soft blue energy from her, something sensitive and nuanced, a little sweetness laced with care and nurturing. *Are you dreaming, Ed?* I ask myself. *You know that wasn't part of the Samantha deal. She is all about fire. And I am all about—well, what am I all about? In spite of everything, I did choose her. If I wanted someone who offered me greater softness and intimacy, wouldn't she be here right now?*

Whoa, the week is already getting intense—and not just from carnal fireworks. This isn't the time to upset things, though. I don't have the strength to face the cost of saying something rash and dislodging our progress south. All this self-reflection will have to wait. *For now, it is business as usual,* I instruct myself.

The next day I try getting oriented by looking at the charts before breakfast. They show the expected: an outside run heading south around Cape Fear to our destination, Bald Head Island, will require at least one overnight sail.

If I wanted someone who offered me greater softness and intimacy, wouldn't she be here right now?

Based on the previous day's experience, it seems we aren't ready for the challenge. It is far less risky to instead pull up anchor and sail back west to Beaufort where we can pick up the Intracoastal. We have five days left, plenty of time to sail leisurely 110 miles on the inland route, leaving perhaps a bit of time for fun when we arrive at Bald Head.

Our first day on the Intracoastal has us into the small town of Swansboro just in time for their Halloween celebration. Quite delightfully for us, this hamlet of brightly painted stucco buildings and tropical plants in terracotta pots has ignored any changes in the outside world since 1955, at least. We find ourselves laughing at the Jalousie storm doors on every house, which neither of us has seen since childhood. The stimulation of early memories is delightful, when life was simpler, and it was possible to leave your front door unlocked. Everything about the décor and the attitude of this quaint town on the Waterway brings us back a good fifty years.

We start out on a walk of the town but soon realize that we're hungry from a full day at sea. Fortunately there is a pleasant dinner spot overlooking the water, adjacent to the marina. Rustic old picnic tables, china and silverware left over from someone's grandmother, all emphasize the sleepy, unpretentious, truly middle-class fifties theme. The food is basic and tasty for sure, but more noteworthy is the skirmish that ensues.

While Samantha is in the restroom, I order a plate of eggplant kebobs as a surprise appetizer. *Nice gesture*, I think, until the little veggie jewels arrive wrapped in bacon. Samantha is vegan. *Bad move, Ed*, but really an innocent mistake, and I assume it will be taken that way. *Good for a laugh*, I think.

Samantha scowls. "Ed, what are you thinking? Do you forget everything about me? That self-centered brain of yours can't get that I don't eat this stuff." Hardly leaving enough space for a breath, she winds up and throws the fastball. "Let me spell it out for you: V-E-G-A-N. And you're supposed to be mister sensitive, wanting to 'relate' all the time. Well, *thank you* for this. At least that slimy wrapping isn't alive."

"Look, sorry. It was supposed to be a treat, but clearly you see it as an attack on your sacred, holy—"

Her eyes are wide and heated. "You can't stand that I don't want to eat all that junk you do."

I'm not giving ground on this one. "It pisses me off that you interpret an innocent mistake as a slight on you. You know I don't eat meat either, so just chill. Maybe you should focus on your reaction instead of on my mistake. Who knows, you might learn something. Damn it, you're hard to please."

"You do please me in several ways," she says, her tone easing. "You know that."

Needing a break from the action, I fake the urge to pee and head off towards the rest room. As I stand over the urinal I think, *Maybe her criticism of me being "mister sensitive" and my "wanting to relate all the time" has something to it. Why do I often play the softer feminine role with her? Damn, where the hell is my masculine?* Oh geez, speaking of masculine (or is it male?) I had better keep my mind on this simple task. She'd surely poke fun if I arrive with wet pants.

On my way back to the table, Mother appears in my mind's eye, just like the other day in the car. My whole body tightens. It's feeling like childhood again. Ugh—the dread feels as alive as ever. I can feel her trying to control my every move with her harsh, overly loud and even scolding voice. It was always about her. I could never please enough. One minute it was deep and intimate, the next it felt like she hated me.

"Ouch," I scream, hitting my head on a low beam, which brings me rudely back into the moment. *It's only Samantha here, not mother,* I tell myself. But I am barely comforted. Connecting the dots is unfortunately getting easier by the moment. I fought off one woman way back in childhood. I'm not going to let another one roll over me now. Damn, the dimensions of this dance with Samantha are bigger than I ever thought. *No kidding, Ed, where have you been?*

We manage to get through the remainder of the meal in one piece. On the way out I pick up the check, as usual, while the sounds of festivity immediately envelop us. In contrast to my inner state, the town celebration is truly joyous as tricksters in a great variety of costumes go from house to house soliciting treats. We join them, which softens us, thank God, literally dancing in the streets to the varied music that emanates from homes, all of which have their doors open in a gesture of warm invitation.

The element of trust is palpable, as if the entire outdoors is communal property. Even the police cars participate in the festivities as officers patrol the neighborhood with cop stereos blaring spooky period tunes through their megaphones. Great fun for an entire town, and at almost eighty degrees it sure beats the chilly Halloween nights I've grown used to up north.

Next morning the yachts peel away from the marina dock one by one, all headed for the same place. They too have done their homework the night before; Wrightsville Beach, approximately sixty Intracoastal miles south, is the most attractive place to anchor for the evening.

As usual, we have compared notes on our analysis with other transient boaters, looking both to confirm our thinking and to pick up any tips from those that have sailed the route before. This is the nightly ritual at marinas, an opportunity not only to gather trip information but also to help create a community of "floaters." Samantha seems to fit right in. She loves the casual nature of the connections, and no one presses her to go deeper. While initially enjoyable, I hope for something closer to the bone. She prefers to stay in motion, while I like to hang with people and get to know them a bit.

Despite our dissimilar styles of connection, Samantha and I manage to find a middle ground that we enjoy together. And, contrary to our usual mode of relating, she and I discuss openly how as a species we seem compelled to build community, even if it is one that itself is on the move. And, more atypically for us, we even muse about the way our dissimilar needs for intimacy get satisfied, or not. *Has the tide shifted, or is this just a curve ball from the universe? I wonder. Are we capable of more than distracting sex?*

After setting anchor in Wrightsville, a very handsome 60-foot ketch (two masts) pulls in next to us. In the process of anchoring, the owners offer the courtesy of asking, "Are we too close?" as good neighbors might. We'd stopped in for a brief visit on Halloween, having noticed that *Finest Kind* was missing its main mast. It was then that the owners—Brad and Sally—recounted the awful story of how they were dismasted while sailing under one of the same railroad bridges Jonah and I went under just south of Norfolk. The bridge had unexpectedly lowered, and despite the terror and physical damage, they decided to continue motoring down the Intracoastal while their main mast—all sixty-five feet of it—was shipped back to its originating boatyard for repairs.

Empathy among strangers is an interesting and even beautiful thing, I am learning.

The story was interesting and provided the glue for us to bond as couples. Now having them next to us for another night feels like meeting up with friends. They are on our port side, while our starboard neighbors are a couple we met just today, and that only via radio contact when seeking advice on bridge openings. Although both connections are circumstantial at best, it is enough to make us feel surrounded by neighbors, bound together by a fascination with sailing, and a mutual concern for the hazards we all must face.

The previous evening we also met a most charming couple—two guys who were sailing a rather small twenty-eight-foot boat. Both of them had a lot of experience and had sailed all the way from Canada, but they were rightfully concerned about the next day's trip to Wrightsville. Their boat, affectionately named *Joda*, could only do five knots. That would mean navigating the last several hours on the Intracoastal in the fading light, and anchoring in Wrightsville amid darkness. We worry about *Joda* and the crew all day. Samantha is particularly vocal, even touchingly sweet (did I say that?), using the VHF radio frequently to see where they are and how they are doing.

Our temporary network of radio buffs is ecstatic when *Joda* finally pulls in a few hours after dark. The entire communal anchorage field lets out a palpable sigh of welcome, made vivid by audible hoots of relief. It amazes and warms me to witness how a sense of caring develops so quickly with relative strangers, most of whom would never come in contact with each other again. Empathy among strangers is an interesting and even beautiful thing, I am learning.

The relationship temperature on board, which I take with great frequency, is surprisingly comfortable. Handing Samantha the wheel in controlled conditions meets her need to take charge while offering me the opportunity to occasionally nap under way. She is competent; there is no question about that. I even allow myself to occasionally think, *As long as I control the sailing conditions, I can control Samantha.*

Ha. I find myself laughing out loud at the absurdity of that notion. It may feel calm in this moment, but I don't trust it. Just like with Mom way back, I never knew when a calm scene would explode, turning instead into a raging firestorm, and for a reason that always evaded me.

Mast/Boom Joint

17
Paradise Imploding

The final day of our trip is a leisurely-thirty mile ride down to Bald Head Island. I chuckle to myself, *it has taken roughly two weeks on the Intracoastal to cover less mileage than Evan, Jonah, and I clocked sailing from Block Island to Norfolk in only three days.* But efficiency is not the objective; instead, having fun, enjoying a leisurely pace, and experiencing interesting locations are what we've been after.

Mission accomplished. Well, sort of. At least I feel rested enough for the final sail to Florida with Jonah. But not before attempting some vacation fun on this resort island and its underwater appendage, Cape Fear. (*Should this ominous name be a warning?*)

Samantha has two days left before she catches a plane back to New Hampshire. Eager to enjoy the remaining time together, I allow myself to think that we will get through the period unscathed. Maybe this will work out after all. Sure there isn't a lot of depth to the connection, but at least the skirmishes have been... *Have been what, Ed?* I ask myself. *Samantha may not have been privy to all that has been going on inside me, but the eruption at Swansboro wasn't exactly a walk in the park. Just because we got over it doesn't mean it didn't happen. And what about my Mother's surprise appearances; wasn't that a clue?* I feel the cloud of self-deception blowing in like a thick and persistent overcast sky.

Bald Head is a unique barrier island with all the fixings: miles of spectacular beaches, untouched woodlands, sand dunes, salt marshes, and tidal creeks. The architecture is discreet and mostly built into the natural surroundings. Food, whether prepared restaurant-style or available in the upscale grocery store, is always first class. Possible activities abound, like walking the beach, kayaking the marshes, or spending quiet time reading and listening to the surf. Cars are not allowed, making peace and quiet a high priority as you get around on easily rented bicycles, electric golf carts, or roller blades. And the weather forecast for our final two days is calling for sunny skies, light winds, and temperatures in the low eighties. Hard to imagine how we could get into any trouble, but we do, and plenty of it.

Our first of two nights comes quickly. We've made dinner reservations at Jason's, one of several restaurants on this island paradise known for its spicy food and original music. Samantha and I talk about our evening together as an "event," perhaps a way of smoothing over any remaining rough spots and maybe even leaping into something new, something deeper. We both seem determined to make this a special moment despite the hard places we've been.

But I don't believe it. Why should I, with our track record? The exchange feels more like avoidance to me than anything else. If a parachute were available, I'd be reaching for it right about now—or would I?

Samantha is finishing buttoning her cream-colored blouse, with hair brushed back and a floral pin in her hair. Her smile is radiant. Struck by how stunning she appears, I tell her, "Honey, you look gorgeous and sexy tonight." Without thinking, I brush my hand gently across her breasts.

She immediately screams, "Keep your damn hands off me." Her face turns wild and her mouth distorts with anger.

I am speechless—the wind knocked out of me. For months we've expressed all kinds of familiarity, so why this violent reaction? Blind with disbelief, and with mounting anger myself, I respond with a verbal jab. "Talk to me like that again and you'll be swimming all the way back to New England," adding, "with your hands tied, and then only if you're lucky." With that I leap off *Kairos* and onto the dock. Spotting a bike propped against a piling I run to it, jump on, and speed off fast. It isn't mine, but I take it anyway. I need to get away from here, and from her, as quickly as possible.

Riding along, I'm still feeling irritated. The degree of it surprises me. I am well-aware of how crazy Samantha's reaction is to my harmless gesture, but why does it affect me so deeply? Why can't I see it for what it is—an exaggerated response by her that has little to do with me—and just walk away? Instead I feel threatened, much like in childhood battles with my mother when there was good reason to fear her intimidating tactics.

Pedaling, pedaling, faster, faster. I keep moving until without warning an image appears. The vision is smoky. There are two faces blended into one—that of Samantha and my mother. Which one is it? *That's it*, I exclaim to myself while hitting a bump and almost crashing into a tree. I'm mistaking one for the other. My reactions to Samantha are, at least in part, mainly outdated responses to my mother. Like Don Quixote swinging at windmills, my fear and resultant anger are misplaced. Samantha may be one hell of a difficult personality to cope with, but she isn't my mother. And I'm not three years old.

The ride continues for at least another hour or so until I'm physically exhausted. My legs ache, and my neck feels spasmodic. It is already dark. I need to return and deal with the aftermath, but I'm scared. I don't trust her (or me) at this point.

Arriving back at the marina, without knowing what awaits me, I take my time proceeding along the dock, step by step, not wanting to rush the impending encounter. Finally, I step aboard

Kairos while holding my breath. Samantha is there to greet me, but surprisingly says little. We both pretend like nothing happened. After making a cup of tea for both of us, more as a stalling tactic than an olive branch, I indicate my need to be alone for the night. *Sleeping in the rear berth by myself with the door closed will give me some degree of safety,* I'm hoping. And maybe some space to further sort this all out. I actually lock the door for the first time.

Emotions are calm the next day, but I can feel the dissonance underneath. The sense of tranquility seems fake, as if we're both waiting for the next eruption from the volcano of love (or is it lust?) to materialize.

And so it does.

It is now the night before Samantha's planned departure. We're preparing dinner together, chopping onions and fennel, when Samantha says to me in a harsh, directive voice, "Don't scrape the knife on the cutting board. Turn the blade over, or use your hand. I've told you that before—don't you ever listen to me? Do we need to send you away to finishing school to learn how to behave?"

I'm shocked and shoot back, equally assertively, "How about, 'Hey, Ed—I'm wondering if doing it like that will dull the knife?'"

"I don't talk like that," she says, eyes widening. "You want everything sugar-coated. I see something I don't like and I say it."

Tigers circling.

"You can be a bitch—you know how to do that real well, don't you?" I say, aware of spinning in a direction I don't like. I've never called a woman a bitch before (at least not to her face). But for me, Samantha is a woman of firsts.

"You don't like anyone who calls you at your game," she says, almost spitting. "You want it all nice-nice, and can't stand the heat." There is a look to her that even I haven't seen before, like a fierce warrior ready for battle. But her expression appears ungrounded and frenetic, like the look of someone about to lose control at any minute. She is scaring me, more, more… "Well, take this mister sweet and sensitive," she says, as she reaches for the long heavy cooking spoon with both hands.

Holding the blunt wooden object first above her head, and then swinging down with force, she begins to inflict damage to the food prep counter. I can't believe my eyes. She is pounding the wood, trashing the beautiful cherry finish. I watch, frozen in disbelief. She is wild, possessed by the force of her action, sweat flying off her, overtaken by her own rage. I watch all this—what feels like the hammering of *me*—cutting right to the place where Samantha and mother merge. I am splitting apart. I can feel her "weapon" cracking open the thick leaden shell around my heart.

It feels like I will surely perish from the pain, but somehow I promptly snap awake from my denial. Then a voice from within says, *This is no dream, Ed, this is real. Act—wake up. ACT NOW.*

I lunge toward her, about to knock her aside and blunt the force of her next blow when all of a sudden she stops. Just stops. Then, further surprising me, her body goes limp and drops the wooden spoon. It is done. She is done. I can feel her releasing whatever demons have gripped her. There is anguish, unresolved grief. I see it flowing out of her like an ugly polluted stream.

With that she pushes me out of the way and moves assertively over to the couch. She appears gone, unreachable and diffuse, like a hurricane without an eye, waiting to reorganize. I'm filled with fear, fists clenched in defense, head spinning, aware of being taken over by a storm of confusion, hurt, and deep sadness.

My heart is thudding, but I'm not sure what to say or do. I usually depend on thinking my way out of things, but only feelings and body sense are available to me now. Something has broken inside me. My rational mind has finally been defeated.

Slow it down, Ed, I beg of myself. *Don't let this unravel any more than it has.* But I am beyond controlling anything; it is all spinning around and around. I try a few deep knee bends—anything to bring the blood back to my brain and help me see more clearly.

I know that something nasty inside me has *also* been released. It feels like an oozing dark paste, like I am bleeding black. Her pounding, pounding, repeated pounding of *Kairos* has cracked open the shell of my resistance. Feeling like a catharsis, the opaque discharge is flowing out, carrying with it the many long-held fears of intimacy that I've kept hidden since childhood.

> *Her pounding, pounding, repeated pounding of Kairos has cracked open the shell of my resistance.*

Stumbling past her to the closet, it is clear that the momentary reprieve is over. She is back, open and ready for more fight. I'm alarmed. *No, no more. Not now,* I say to myself as I hastily throw a few clothes in an available bag. *Whatever is going on inside of me, I need space to let it happen. Get out of here now, Ed.*

Intentionally avoiding any eye contact, I reach around Samantha to grab my bag, leap out of *Kairos*, and run down the dock as quickly as I can. My hands shake. By the time I reach the end of the dock, I realize I am crying.

Breathe, Ed, breathe, I say to myself with assertion. *Please, get some control over yourself.* I am relieved to be out of Samantha's range, but my head doesn't work. I'm not sure what to do next. Desperate for clarity, I put my head between my legs and try breathing deeply again. This is all I can do. This is all I can do.

Finally, after what seems like an eternity of sitting on the dirty curb, I pick myself up and begin to walk. But I'm feeling woozy—not sensing my feet hitting the pavement. I can't feel anything except the fear. More deep breathing. More shaking. More tears. *Just keep going, Ed,* I say. *You remember, one foot in front of the other. That is all you need to do. Breathe, step, breathe, step.*

Then, a familiar sign up ahead: The Harbor Hotel. I've passed it before, even laughed at the ridiculously expensive prices. But I don't care. I just want shelter. Damn the cost. What I need now is space, and some perspective. I need to hide. To be protected by my aloneness.

The clerk at the check-in desk looks at me like I'm crazy—hair wild, eyes blurry, arm gestures erratic. But she hands me the room key anyway after I scribble my name on the credit card voucher. *Is this for real?* I say to myself. *Am I really spending the night in a hotel with* Kairos *just a half mile away? What the hell, man? What has your life turned into?*

Once in the safety of the room, I double lock the door and flop onto the bed. Lying there, with the moment swirling around me, I hear her voice wanting to cut into me. I don't have to close my eyes; there she is, pounding *Kairos* over and over, exacting the blood of her childhood. The violence, the venom she inflicts is all about killing off her demons. She never let me in close enough to know them. But there they all are, being beheaded now, one by one by one. It feels deep and old, like longstanding wounds she sustained from others whose exorcism is long overdue.

Running into the bathroom, I splash my face with cold water, then hot, then cold. I try running in place, then more alternations of hot and cold water. I need more perspective, more presence of mind, and more equanimity to deal with all of this.

I was just in the wrong place at the wrong time. Or was it the right place at the right time? Was she wielding the cudgel for both of us? Besides killing off her own demons, it now seems clear that the sheer force of her destruction was doing double duty, killing off *mine* as well.

I pull my knees into my chest. Back and forth, back and forth, the feeling is beginning to come into my body again. Slowly, slowly, I can feel my blood resuming its flow once more.

Ah...deep breath...shoulders release. I feel my chest lighten. My breathing, though jagged, is getting easier. Something is shifting in me, becoming less protective, softer. There are tears—I am crying again—sobbing, really. I feel naked, as though the protective coating has finally let go, discharging six or so decades of pent-up pain and agony. It is all flowing now—years and years of deep pain. There is shame, harshness, and a lack of love in childhood, but it is flowing out of me, not stuck inside. I've kept it hidden for so long, and it's been oh so painful, like being behind bars and locked in my own childhood prison.

More clarity floods in. I can see how desperately I tried to be good. To be the best at everything, just for a few scraps of love. There is a deep ache of vulnerability. I feel it underneath like an uncovered wound. Exposing it would have hurt too much. That's why I always picked safe intimate partners, ones who were more like friends than lovers. I couldn't tolerate the instability that would have come from exposing a badly bruised heart. I just wanted to be loved, but I was too frightened to let go into it.

Yet here I am, right at the flash point of my life. Now is the time to face my truth head on, to stick my entire being into the head of the dragon. To know that I can tolerate even *that*.

I'm feeling better, but still a bit like a conductor-less train. Calming, calming—I move toward the TV in the corner chest, push the power button, and up flashes a Red Sox game. Not ironically, the picture sharpens just as one of our hometown sluggers hits a walk off grand slam. Opening the room refrigerator I grab a bag of nuts and a bottle of water.

The distraction doesn't last long. Shutting down the TV she is there again, but more at a distance now. There is spaciousness too— not as much in my face, or as scary. It seems her continued presence is forcing me

It is time to heal; time to love. It is time to risk all for the sake of connectivity— real connectivity.

to face the reality of my own wounded nature, and to embrace that the thing I long for most—intimacy—has been blocked by my own reactivity and defensiveness. This self-honesty feels good, and further calms me.

It is time to heal, time to love again. I hear this over and over in the chambers of my heart. *It is time to heal, time to love. It is time to risk all for the sake of connectivity—real connectivity.*

My heartbeat is slowing. My fear is decreasing, even though the pain inside is like a hot knife searing my delicate skin. And the grief, there is that too, as I feel into what I have forfeited over all these years—life with an authentic connection; life with the vitality that only intimacy can bring. I'm beginning to sense some degree of reconciliation, some degree of freedom—maybe even tranquility. And as I do I can feel my heart. Yes, *feel my heart.* Now that is new.

Like sailing out of the fog, my way forward begins to emerge from the haze. I can see a new Ed, a guy who can step gently and fully into his masculinity; a strong, sensitive male capable of holding the feminine with his heart open. There is greater freedom in his gait as he steps away from fighting his mother's endless fight. He is in the future, but I can see him. And he is happy. Peaceful.

Glancing at the clock, it is way past 1 a.m., but I feel lighter and more rested than I have in over fifty years. There is so much more to come, so much more to process. But for now my state of peacefulness is drifting me into sleepiness. My eyes close as I feel held. It was there all along, this pure, unconditional love. I just had to clear my channels and open to it.

Amazingly, I sleep the entire night through, held tenderly by the deep stillness. I feel safe, as though someone pushed the stop switch and I no longer have to continue this tortuous ride. That beautiful

He is in the future, but I can see him. And he is happy. Peaceful.

reservoir of feminine ocean energy has finally come to the rescue. It softened and held me as Samantha stripped away my defenses—a productive conspiracy of opposites. Together, like the melding of fire and water, they worked to enable the release of my defenses while forcing my own truth to emerge. *So that was the real reason for going to the sea and for this relationship with Samantha,* I muse with a smile on my face.

The following day, neither one of us seems eager to process anything, and I'm clearly not ready to pull the final ripcord. Samantha may need to go, but I've learned that it's not about her anyway.

I feel exhausted from fifty years of hard lessons crammed into one evening, even with a good following sleep. Who knows what Samantha is feeling? For sure, I'm not interested in finding out. And she asks no questions, so we remain pleasant to each other with both of us already distracted by the

So that was the real reason for going to the sea and for this relationship with Samantha...

life we are going back to once the other leaves the perimeter. There is a palpable sense that our relationship is over, without the finality of acknowledgement; that this dance has run its course, served its usefulness. We just need to find the appropriate time and place to issue the final goodbye.

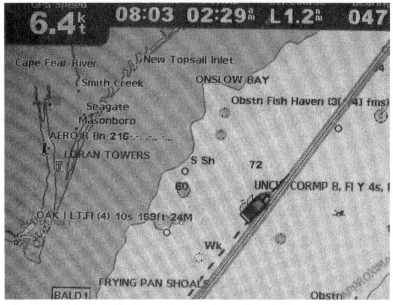

Cape Fear On the GPS

18
The Inevitable

Jonah arrives at the Wilmington airport only a few hours after Samantha's departure. Following a warm, enthusiastic two-way greeting, we immediately begin to address all necessary preparations for the final leg of the sail south. There is just enough time to purchase food for our five-to-seven-day trip, drop off the rental car, and hail a taxi to make the 8:30 ferry to Bald Head Island. I'm hoping this will get us to bed by 10, allowing sufficient time to secure a decent night's sleep before leaving early the next morning. After all, we have in front of us at least three full days and nights on the open ocean without a break.

I try hard to clear my mind of Samantha, but she haunts me. There are so many unanswered questions, so much work to be done. *Ya gotta love it,* I think. Just a few months ago I thought I was getting this sexy, smart, uncomplicated life partner to sail off into the sunset with, and now it appears that she was sent from the universe to illuminate the pathway of my own rocky self recovery. Gee, what kind of fun is that? Maybe it's time to put through an inquiry to the Zen Center and see if they have any long-term rooms available.

I think about phoning her from the ferry, but decide not to. Then the phone rings. Her number flashes on my screen. Do I answer it?

"Ed, hi, is that you?" she asks almost softly. "I just got back to Prescott a few minutes ago and wanted to catch up. I know tomorrow will be a demanding day for you, but, well, I just need to feel some degree of closure after what happened."

At first I'm taken aback. Samantha hardly ever calls me, and her voice is uncharacteristically yielding. After a bit more, the softness in her voice begins to sound fake—more like a deceptive prelude to the kill scene.

"Yeah, sure, it's me. Jonah and I are on our way back to Bald Head. You remember the ferry. And how was your trip back north?" I'm saying all of this while trying to find a little privacy on an overstuffed boat. Some passengers flee from me for more isolation of their own, some move closer, sensing a juicy (albeit one-sided) scene.

She jumps back in, staying right on point, now with a sense of dogged persistence. "So, Ed, I've been thinking that maybe this is a good time to put a period at the end of our dance. You know, like maybe we've run the course and it's time to throw in the proverbial towel."

I can feel the heat building in her. The fire is beginning to pour out my end of the phone. *Now this is more like the Samantha I know*, I think to myself.

"I mean, we've had some amazing times, off the chart really, but I just can't take any more of these swings. One minute we're flying, and the next we're crashing. I'm not about to change, and neither are you."

Whoa, I'm not sure if it's me or the ferry that is rockin' and rollin', but something is moving. And then—

"Frankly, I'm tired of all the drama. I like you well enough, and perhaps there are some lessons to be learned, but Jesus you can be overly sensitive and reactive at times." I can feel her winding up to deliver the knockout punch.

"Never have I lost control like what you provoke in me. Maybe you were right. Despite all the good things, our energies just insist on being combative. And I for one am tired of it all. I want out—now."

Ouch. Double ouch. Even though I knew it was coming, I still can't believe this is taking place, and on the ferry no less. Did she say she wanted out? Is it really over? Part of me wants to explode back at her; part of me knows it is a gift I should accept graciously. I catch my breath and, surprising myself, respond from a place of relative calm.

"I've been thinking the same thing, Samantha, but wasn't sure how or when to talk about it." I hear my heart beating. "I should have known I could rely on your feistiness to slam the door shut—and right in my face. Subtlety isn't your middle name." *Keep going, Ed. Now, now,* I say to myself. *This is it. Do it now.*

"So yes, I do think it is time for us to call it quits, to embrace what appears like the inevitable. It saddens me deeply, and I know there will be more of that pain later, but I do think it is the right action. We need to admit it doesn't work, and let go."

"Good," she chuckles, "maybe we can finally agree on something. OK, it is getting late and I know…"

"Wait," I say, "there is more. Don't hang up yet." I can feel that ripping feeling in my heart. Can she really be that callous, even now? This may be the right thing to do, but it hurts like hell. I search for restraint, wanting to come out of this with some degree of dignity.

"Look, Sam, I'm really sorry for my part in all of this—for hurting you, for hurting me. I know I can be defensive at times. I just wish I'd been a better partner for you. I'm more aware now of what I need to do, but that will have to be with someone else, or alone."

"Gee, Ed, I didn't think you had that in you. Oh, and I probably played some small part in the dissonance, also," she says with an obvious smile in her voice.

Taking a breath...

"Sam, I'll miss you. Despite all the head-butting, there is just something about us that is pretty special. I wish you well and will take many fond memories of you with me." (*I want to say I love you, but it isn't true. That is the saddest truth of all.*)

"Yes, you too, Ed. Be well, and as Garrison says, stay above average."

At that very moment the ferry, pulling into the dock, lets out a huge blast from its horn as if in celebration. Following up quickly on the cue, I press the END key on my phone, and the connection is severed. Passengers start moving off the ship while I sit there stunned. *Did that really happen,* I ask myself? And I mean not just that exchange, but the whole bloody affair. The whole bloody affair.

After a gentle nod from one of the ferry's workers, I begin to move slowly toward the exit. Jonah is up ahead. I wave him off and indicate that we'll meet back at *Kairos*, while I find a bench to sit on. Allowing my feelings free reign, I gradually come back into the moment and begin feeling centered again.

It feels like the tide has turned, the current now flowing more in than out. I feel freer, more alive, and more whole. Yet I also feel a deep sense of loss and sadness for the dissipation of the dream—the dream of finding a mate with whom to experience joy in life while sailing off into the sunset together. That isn't going to be the script after all, at least not this time.

Negotiating With the Tankers

19
Staying Afloat

After walking around the island for a few hours, I somehow find my way back to *Kairos*. I'm in a daze, but a comfortable one, more oriented than disoriented. Despite the sting of finality, I know we did the right thing. *Hindsight will help make sense of it all*, I tell myself. For now, I'm okay with just moving forward, and glad that it's Jonah who's sleeping on *Kairos* tonight.

"Hey Cap, what the hell happened to you? And *Kairos*, shit, looks like this cherry counter got beat up real bad. Are you okay?"

"Yeah, I don't want to get into it much right now. We have a long sail ahead of us, and I'd rather not be any more distracted than I already am." Taking a deep breath, and pausing a bit to catch up with my thoughts, I continue, "Let's just say both *Kairos* and I went through the eye of the storm. She came through it with her countertop torn up bad, and I feel like my heart took a really violent pounding. But, overall, I'm feeling like it was a good thing, something that needed to be done, and something that released me to move on, lighter and feeling more free."

Having never seen this side of me, Jonah stumbles to respond in his usual detached surfer-boy manner. "Yeah man, wow, that's heavy duty. Let's hope the sea treats us better than that over the next few days," he offers, sporting a wry grin.

With that I hand Jonah a beer, something he never turns down. We toast to the mystery of the feminine, vowing to stay a safe distance. But both of us know it's all much more complex, and that neither one of us will stay away for very long.

By midnight we are in bed, he perhaps surfing the ocean blue in his dreams, while I dive into the comfort of all that feminine ocean energy—alone again, and glad for it.

The next morning we're on our way by 8 a.m. with favorable weather predictions. But despite the blue skies and gentle wind, Captain Ed is nervous. I begin to seriously second-guess my decision to venture out with only one crew member—especially since I am still exhausted from the week just past.

Up to this point I've executed only one ocean leg as captain: the trip from Block Island to Norfolk. On that sail, which is of similar distance, there were two crew members, including the expert help of Evan. On this leg—North Carolina to Florida—Jonah is it, requiring that we alternate three-hour shifts throughout the night. And with Jonah a relatively inexperienced crewmate, the burden of strategic decisions will be entirely on my shoulders. Even making routine sail changes, or engaging in other maneuvers that require both of us, will further compromise sleep time. My stamina at sixty-three for this level of physical stretch is becoming increasingly limited. Should I do it? Am I letting my emotional need to complete the trip outweigh important considerations of safety—both mine and Jonah's?

We toast to the mystery of the feminine, vowing to stay a safe distance. But both of us know it's all much more complex, and that neither one of us will stay away for very long.

Still haunted with doubt, I make the decision to depart. Then, in less than a half-hour we are facing the first few challenges: a mild but opposing current that will temporarily slow us down, and a fleet of large commercial freighters coming right at us on their way up to Wilmington. This is morning rush hour on the ocean. Imagine being in a thirty-six-foot sailboat with a dozen or so six-hundred-foot (or more) vessels headed right at you. Sure makes my blood feel like ice water. Fortunately, there is room to navigate outside the channel, and I'm certainly not going to argue with these guys. I keep *Kairos* well off to their starboard, where there is enough deep water, and everybody's happy (I'm hoping).

Likely the most important decision I will make over the next few days is where to point *Kairos*. That is, where on the Florida coast are we going to make landfall? If you're not a sailor, this seems like a pretty straightforward exercise, yet it's anything but.

Our ultimate destination is Cocoa Village, located at mile marker 897.5 on the Intracoastal. The previous June/July, while waiting six weeks for *Kairos* to be ready, I had scouted out marinas, thinking it likely I would return to this area at least for part of the winter. The principal advantage would be access to my family's little-used condominium. Plus, I had made serious connections in the Cocoa Beach community that last year, especially the alternative spiritual fringe of it.

Choosing Cocoa Village as a destination means getting back onto the Intracoastal at some point. We can take the inland waterway for the entire trip, but that would require approximately ten days—a long slog down the "ditch." Instead, if we stay outside until Jacksonville—the northern-most deep-water inlet in Florida with access to the Intracoastal—my estimate shows us arriving only six days later. For now, Jacksonville is it.

Ah, it feels so good to be back out on the ocean again with uninterrupted views in every direction. For me there is a quality of expansiveness that I feel nowhere else: a sense of deep spiritual connection. Outside of the obvious dangers of ocean sailing, it is here that I am happiest, and feel more reconciled, than anywhere else on earth. Plus the energy between Jonah and me continues to be good. He has such an easygoing nature and is always willing and eager to help with any sailing task.

Day one continues from its blissful start, with the weather cooperating every step of the way. Even with an initially unfavorable current, we are able to maintain an average speed of six knots. But by the beginning of the second day the wind shifts, coming around to our stern. That drops our speed to 4.5 knots. Besides slowing us down, steering *Kairos* with the wind from behind can be dangerous, especially with a relatively inexperienced crewmate at the helm. Even a minor shift in wind direction from this position can provoke an uncontrolled jibe and, in the worst of cases, lead to a dismasting. Clearly I have to come up with a different strategy, and fast.

"Hey Jonah, wake up. I know you've been crunching it for the past two days, but I need another brain to help me figure."

Meanwhile, the wind and resultant surf have been building, occasionally coming over the transom and into the cockpit. I am beginning to look like the great salt monster from the deep blue.

"So here's the deal, man. I'm thinking of changing course. We're getting blown all around. This tack is downright dangerous. Plus we've lost a lot of speed, and I'm reluctant to turn on the engine."

I have to almost shout because of the howling wind and the pitching boat. "How 'bout I turn this puppy about thirty degrees to the south and head right for Ponce De Leon Inlet? I know we're tired and changing direction will add fifteen hours to the ocean part of the trip…" Jonah looks as engaged as a snail on a mountaintop, but I carry on. "But it would also shave off twenty-six hours from the total, plus save us two days of motoring on the Intracoastal. Hey, hold that thought for a minute, this surf is rattling my kidneys—I need to pee."

As I stand on the leeward side of *Kairos*, holding tight with only one hand available, I'm tossed in every direction. My aim is not good—I hope not a harbinger of what's to come.

"Okay, I'm back," I tell Jonah, who stands wet and tired at the wheel. "The big risk is getting there after dark, and my best case has us arriving at three in the afternoon—only a three hour cushion before darkness sets in. We don't want to spend all night in eight-foot seas while waiting for the next morning's light."

I wait for his reply.

"Jonah, are you listening? Are you following me? This is big stuff, man, and I really need some input from you."

"Hey I'm listening, Captain. But it's damn hard while getting blown all around out here."

I can see Jonah is not going to be of much use on this one. His passivity, appreciated greatly after Samantha's in-your-face style, isn't what I need just now. And he seems to avoid anything resembling a calculation, or an opinion. Maybe my flattering assessment of his laid back style is a bit romanticized? So I forget about his input and choose between the better of two not-very-good options, reprogram the GPS, turn the wheel thirty degrees to the left, and immediately get religious.

The remainder of our trip is arduous and wet, but at exactly 3 p.m., two days after making the decision, we head into the Ponce De Leon Inlet. It was one hell of a fast sail (upwards of seven knots at times), and a salty one at that.

As I imagined, the entrance is tricky, even during daylight. Inlets on the Florida coast are a constant work in progress, with shifting bottom conditions waiting to snag sailboats and their deep keels. Guided by the help of recently reset buoys, we successfully thread our way through the dangerous sections, but not without serious heart palpitations on my part. Once in, and safely on the Intracoastal, we head directly south and pull into the first available marina.

I can hardly believe it. Here we are, comfortably tied to a sheltered dock with only fifty protected miles ahead of us to Cocoa Village. It would be an understatement to say that I am exhausted. I do manage to put together a modest dinner, take a shower, and clean up the boat a bit. Up to this point my mind has been blissfully free from thoughts of Samantha—good or bad. The challenges of the trip took priority. But I know that as soon as we reach Cocoa the next day, memories of her will come flooding back.

After I fall into the sack, Jonah leaves for the evening and doesn't arrive back until after 2 a.m. "So what's up, Jonah?" I say, seeing him stumbling around, but half asleep myself. "What the hell happened? You're acting like you've been hit by a truck. Tomorrow's a big day—the weather channel predicts thirty-knot winds."

"Uh, yeah man," he mutters while heading toward his bunk. "I'll be ready. Late night—could have been worse. Woman picked me up at the bar… took me home. Wanted me to stay… I said no…" His voice trails off. "I'll be ready."

I hope so, because he isn't getting any sympathy from me. Drifting back to sleep, I think, *Jonah's immature, but I do envy the guy at times.* I also know that maturity is subjective, and often overrated, especially when you're over sixty.

The forecast turns out to be accurate. The wind blows all day between 28–32 knots. Even though the Intracoastal affords us protection from high surf, it is a wild and wooly ride. Thank goodness Jonah and I already had our exchange over my need for his help.

By mid-afternoon we arrive at Cocoa Village, tired but smiling. The segment from Bald Head Island has taken an amazingly short four-and-a-half days. To think that just four weeks prior I'd been on Cape Cod, mired in ambiguity, and barely able to decide whether to embark on the trip, or not.

Our arrival in Cocoa on November 8, 2009 leaves me feeling buoyant and celebratory. After all, today marks the completion of my first sail south as captain of *Kairos*, with no casualties or even serious problems along the way. The trial has gone well—much better than expected. All the prep work from last summer paid big dividends. Sitting in the warm Florida sun on a deck one story above *Kairos*, I muse. *What will be the next chapter of this unfolding journey into the unknown?*

In All Her Glory

20

So What Was
That All About?

Reflecting Back

The years just prior to my sea journey were tough. It all came to a head in 2007 when I was closing in on sixty-one—time to kick back and reap the hard-earned rewards of a life well-lived, or at least that is what the greater culture would have had me believe back then. Instead, I felt caught in the uncomfortable and even painful swirl of a life defined by ambiguity. With my business sold, and endless unstructured time on my hands, I had little sense of what to do with my life, or what to engage in that would feel meaningful.

My identity during the middle years, or roughly the prior two and a half decades, had been based primarily on external forms of recognition. I was a father, a spouse, and a well-paid executive at work. That is how I defined myself. And the larger culture reinforced the message by saying repeatedly, and in myriad ways, hooray for you. Then, in what seemed like an instant, my marriage unraveled, my son went off to college, and I retired from full-time work. Yikes—I didn't know who I was anymore. It seemed like everything had been taken away—or worse, that I had bet my life on a good hand, and lost.

Sensing despair, a friend tried to help by sending along a short exercise designed to assess which lifelong dreams still held energy for me. The questionnaire suggested I first identify aspirations for the next ten years, and then asked what I would regret not having done were I to have only twenty-four hours to live. "At your age, given an ever-shortening time horizon, the two lists should be nearly identical," he said. They weren't.

I had little sense of what to do with my life, or what to engage in that would feel meaningful.

This quick inquiry illuminated how, left to my own devices, I would likely continue to delay important life choices, all justified by the assumption that there was plenty of time. But would I really be in good enough physical and mental shape to address some of those important dreams in my seventies, then only nine years away, not to mention my eighties? Was I instead running out of good healthy time? And would this be my final wakeup call?

I did produce a list of must-do intentions that, with a little work, reduced down to two items: grow more inwardly spiritual (which embraced activities such as making more music and developing a steady meditation practice), and engage in more blue-water sailing. No surprise—the two were mutually reinforcing. Over time I came to realize what my

It seemed like everything had been taken away—or worse, that I had bet my life on a good hand, and lost.

spirit knew all along, that living on the water held the potential to address both the concrete and the intangible, a deep connection to the ocean, and a boost in consciousness. I could see then that arriving at my deathbed without having at least attempted the dream of long-distance sailing was unacceptable, even if I ended up not liking it. In my view, the only failure would be not having tried.

I resisted a change of that magnitude though, at least initially. Selling my house, moving out of the safety of my community, and entering a totally undefined world of living on a boat seemed too overwhelming. The emptiness of it scared me. I knew my life required a shift in orientation from outward to inward. But I was caught ill-prepared to source my identity from within, having relied upon external validation most of my life.

Was I instead running out of good healthy time? And would this be my final wakeup call?

Compounding the predicament, I was going to have to do it alone, without a partner to accompany me—no one to cushion the blow of feeling at times irrelevant, lost, and lonely. The combination of large doses of emptiness laced with loneliness—even if only occasional—felt like a toxic recipe to be avoided back then; but the trap had been set, and there seemed no way out but through, even though the steps to take were far from clear.

The emptiness of it scared me.

After years of being a *somebody* (mostly in concert with my wife Catherine), I had overnight become a *nobody*.

Skipping Ahead to the Present

Yet here I am, only several years later, having completed a successful round-trip sail of the East Coast of America. I wouldn't have believed that was possible a few years ago. And along the way I experienced a fiery romance, a deepening bond with my only son, and the blaze of self-transformation.

There has been progress in spiritual matters as well. While harder to quantify, I feel freer and better reconciled to embrace whatever challenges lie ahead. My fear of emptiness has diminished, even to the point where I often draw strength and comfort from moving into it. And I am better equipped to embrace my aloneness.

Standing at the marina dock, I'm reminded of the poignant phrase "Today is a good day to die," which I've always interpreted to mean: at this moment I am at a deep enough reconciliation point in life that if I died today, all would be well. And that is exactly how I feel.

There will be much time for continued reflection and personal growth over the winter months, but for now I need to attend to a few immediate practical concerns like activating phone and Internet connections at the condo, registering my car in Florida, and securing a Florida driver's license. All part of becoming legitimate on land as well as out at sea.

> ... at this moment I am at a deep enough reconciliation point in life that if I died today, all would be well.

Within a week I am live electronically and back to something resembling my Cocoa Beach routine from the prior summer. For exercise there are yoga classes every day, along with four-to-five-mile walks on the beach, and I've taken steps to become better integrated into the alternative spiritual community. Given the steadiness of a land base, I also begin to invest time in documenting my journey to the sea.

At first I had recorded my move from Foster, and the subsequent sailing trip with occasional notes, relying purely on serendipitous flashes of inspiration. But as the weeks wore on, I wrote with increased frequency. Those early note-takings were the seeds, but the idea of writing this book emerged only recently, and from a most unexpected source.

Oh how I love my Saturday morning meditation classes with Manny. From the first clap of his wooden Zen blocks, my mind begins to focus.

"Easy is right," he says in his resonant tenor voice. "If it's right, it's easy."

Each week he leads with that pithy phrase, and each week I find deeper meaning in it. We start with Chi Gong flow exercises to bring the energy into our bodies, and then move into either one long, or two shorter meditation sits. In our newly acquired transcendent state, Zen Master Manny then presides over an elegant tea ceremony.

After class we all receive our clean-up assignments. For the first class, my task is to wash out the teapot and cups with the help of a co-meditator. Of course she is blonde and curvy, which I notice even in my ethereal, post-meditated state.

"So, whatcha doin' here?" she blurts out while handing me a washed cup to dry.

Taken aback by her folksy style, I feel there is some sort of message for me, so I keep drying the cup, avert my eyes, and respond. "I've just sailed down from Massachusetts. And a few months before that, I sailed up from Florida."

"Wow, that sounds romantic," she says, nodding and adding, "even provocative."

She meant the trips, but for a moment I imagine she is referring to herself. As I finish up the drying she says, "Well, I sure hope you are writing this all down. *You know, like a book or something.*"

Funny, I never see her again, even though I attend every Saturday class Manny offers in the following six months. But she did her job as a messenger from the universe, or at least that is what I take her to be.

Writing this book is now an indispensable part of my daily routine—the medium through which I seek to better understand what I lived through over the past several years. It helps me comprehend who I am, and how I got here. It is the essential introspective activity that aids in the clarification and integration of the new me, one now sourced primarily from internal reference points.

In addition to my daily writing sessions, *Kairos* is a convenient five miles away. I regularly enjoy leisurely day sails or spur-of-the-moment adventures. She keeps me connected to the energy of the sea while I continue to listen for clues on what broad directions to consider next. Forget any long-term plan, though—this is time to tune in and follow. Of course I still have dreams, aspirations, and a vague vision of the future, but I seem uninterested in developing (much less following) a detailed map. Most of the time, I am content to be right here and in the moment.

Writing this book… is the essential introspective activity that aids in the clarification and integration of the new me, one now sourced primarily from internal reference points.

"Hi Mom, yeah it's good to hear your voice also. And thanks, I too feel good about completing the trip."

She allows the exchange of pleasantries to continue only briefly before pulling it back to her motherly refrain. "Binky, you're not alone are you? Do you have companionship?"

Gee, not that again, I think. I quickly change the subject and offer something that will be momentarily reassuring to her. But Mother's return to the loneliness theme triggers me. I'm certainly better reconciled to going it alone then I used to be, but not completely. And I haven't entirely let go of the dream of sailing into the sunset with a woman at my side.

"Binky, are you there?"

ED MERCK

"Oh, Mom, sure, I'm here—just daydreaming a bit. You know me. Listen, I've got to run—the cable guy will be here in a minute to install my Internet connection."

"Well I hope I see you before I *go*," she says in an uncharacteristically wistful tone.

Not able to fully absorb the poignancy but knowing all too well what she is talking about, I respond somewhat tongue-in-cheek with, "So, where are you *going*, Mom?"

"You know, *going, going*," she says emphatically. "After all, I'm already past the ninety-year-old mark."

"Oh that," I say, feeling the clutch in my heart. "Well before you do, it's been a while since I've told you, uh, how much I love you. Lots, Mom, lots." I'm a little taken aback at my openness and my unguarded voice of vulnerability. But it feels good, and perfectly natural. Ever since the healing moment on Bald Head Island, my love for Mom just flows, unabated.

"This lifetime of ours hasn't been the easiest for either of us. There were moments when I'd have rather strangled than hugged you, and I'm sure you felt the same." *Is this really me talking?* I wonder. My heart feels so open. It's so good to be here.

"I sure am grateful you outlived all your friends, Mom. We needed the time to get back into each other. To find out how much alike we really are, and how much we really love each other down deep." *Oh my god,* I think, *here it comes.* "These last few years have been precious. I'll never forget the sweetness of feeding you after your hip surgery—we came full circle on that one, didn't we? You're one hell of a gutsy woman, Mom, and I'm sure glad I've got your genetic code running through my veins." With that my eyes moisten. The joy is flowing now, surprising even me. I can feel it throughout my entire body.

"I feel the same, Binky. I am so proud that you are my son—and my firstborn at that. I still can't figure you out, but I love you with all my heart."

A Few Scars, but Much Wiser

21
Becoming the Instrument

Spring 2010

It's now been a few months since Samantha's departure and the conclusion of my successful sail south. Life feels different. Along with some lingering sadness from the collapse of the dream, and the related loss of my co-conspirator, there is a new surge of energy. Each day I grow increasingly content with living alone. Life itself has become my steady partner.

Life itself has become my steady partner.

The more reconciled my internal reality becomes, the more self-acceptance I generate. Quite naturally I've begun to live from that place more often as my mind seeks out commonality. All men have begun to feel like my brothers, all women my sisters. Even the birds, fish, and trees—all living beings—feel like part of the same wildly diverse but close-knit family. I am perfectly happy to define myself these days more as a part of something, than as one of the parts.

I am perfectly happy to define myself these days more as a part of something, than as one of the parts.

I've had lots of time to reflect on Samantha and the impact of that sprightly, energetic blonde who bounded off the ferry some eight months ago. There is no point denying her importance in my ongoing transformation to a more integrated masculine presence. She helped me see a more truthful version of myself, and she helped me heal the wounds of childhood trauma. Most importantly, she cracked open the shell of defensiveness around my heart, making it possible for me to love, and to be intimate again.

It is now time to fully stand in my own two shoes, time for me to take responsibility for my own emotional life, and time for me to be my own source of spiritual connection and unconditional love.

Then, one day in late March, 2010, after a particularly deep meditation class, I find my way to the Tree of Life Rejuvenation Center website, a highly respected wellness retreat enclave in the Arizona desert. Many of my fellow yoga students speak favorably of this well-body oasis whose focus is raw cuisine, meditation, and yoga. Right there on the homepage is a prophetic quote from its director, Dr. Gabriel Cousens, which nearly leaps off the page at me: "...you have to love yourself enough to want to heal yourself, to want to reach for a higher quality of life."

The phrase strikes like a bolt of intuition. After months of allowing body, mind, and spirit to find a new equilibrium point, I now feel ready to reengage my journey and reach out yet again on the rocky path to greater wholeness. Seven days after first looking at the website, I am in Patagonia, Arizona for their Twenty-One-Day Rejuvenation Retreat.

Arriving at the Tucson airport around noon on check-in day I am greeted by the prearranged cab driver who is to chauffeur me to Patagonia, but not before picking up another "camper" who arrived the evening before. As we pull up to the hotel entrance, out springs a lively blonde female. *Oh no, not another*, I think. This woman is drop-dead gorgeous, twenty years my junior, and filled with enough life force to power the hour-long cab ride all the way to the Tree.

She flips her suitcase into the trunk and swings in next to me on the backseat. "Hi, I'm Jan from Oklahoma," she says, extending her firm yet unmistakably feminine hand. Less than five minutes later, as my mind races with visions of dancing sugarplums, she says, "So, are you up for the enemas? You know, our morning colon cleansing?" I gasp at the incongruity between my already well-developed fantasies of this woman, and what has just come out of her mouth.

Regaining my composure—sort of—I say with a grin, "I hadn't realized they were on the menu." She proceeds to fill me in on what the next three weeks will hold for us. I came to Arizona on pure instinct, now I'm beginning to wonder if a little advance research would have kept me, more appropriately, back in Florida.

In fact, there are plenty of new and often jarring experiences over the next three weeks. Morning enemas and frequent colonics during week one are just the beginning. I find little energy for any follow-up fantasies about Jan, or any other women. For now it is all about cleaning out and tuning up this faithful vessel that has carried me through life thus far.

The big new experience for me is the centerpiece of week one: a juice fast. Yippee. I have never experienced the pleasure of fasting, despite hanging out in various spiritually oriented places over the years; curious, maybe, but the energy to fully engage hasn't ever surfaced. Well

Can it be that the price of becoming free is simply letting go?

here I am, having paid big bucks for the privilege of not eating for eight days. And Jan is correct. It isn't good enough to just stop the flow of food and allow the body to naturally detox, we have to actively clean out the entire digestive/elimination canal with some serious scrubbing. I learn that sixty-three years of accumulated living paints no pretty picture.

In addition to yoga, meditation, walking, dharma talks, and spiritual ceremony, we drink—oh so slowly—a pint of nutrient-rich vegetable juice multiple times each day, made from the freshest vegetables available. Each jar of green liquid is the product of a few heads of kale, several cucumbers, sprouts of multiple kinds, perhaps a handful of celery, and any other fresh veggies (preferably green) that are hanging around looking to be consumed (of course, organic only). Our big treat comes when the staff juicer surprises us by throwing in some beets or a carrot. Nothing solid, but all we need to nourish our "temples" back to a more vibrant state of health.

This exercise in detox is a challenge for me both physically and emotionally. It is my time to pay for all the past overindulgences. Each day I feel the impurities oozing out of me in the form of headaches, skin rashes, and their emotional cousins—frightful dreams and anxiety. Gradually I begin to see how many of my habits of consumption are just outdated patterns, some to fuel my unhealthy striving for achievement, others to help conceal my fears.

Then, another epiphany. With assistance from our process, I realize that most of my unhealthy thought forms are just that, thought forms, which *I have created*. They are merely stories I have invented and repeatedly tell myself. There is nothing absolute about them. They only provide a temporary sense of security, something needed to survive childhood. Now, fifty years later, they are a weight dragging me down, or sludge blocking me up. Stories like, *I am only deserving of love if I continue to achieve at an ever-increasing level*, or the really big one: *the problem is out there, not in here.*

With this realization comes power. Since I have created these stories, I can just as easily release them (well, maybe not quite as easily). Can it be that the price of becoming free is simply letting go?

ED MERCK

"Think about that," I say to myself out loud. This is truly revelatory. If I take full responsibility for my stories—most of which no longer serve me, and many of which are a limiting notion of whom I really am—life itself will be more available. Spirit will be less encumbered in its pursuit of truth as

I learn that my life's work is not to play the instrument, rather, to become the instrument.

experienced through my being. In the words of the Persian poet Rumi, "We are lutes, no more, no less." I learn that my life's work is not to *play* the instrument, rather, to *become* the instrument.

And here I am in the middle of a desert. What's with that—I thought this was a journey about sailing? Maybe even sailing's been just a metaphor all along; the real journey toward wholeness is, for each of us, an inside job.

I had no idea how this year of intense transition and personal growth would evolve when I set sail. At times it was scary, especially when I realized there wasn't even a destination to be had, merely an unfolding process. For sure, there were plenty of risks, like abruptly stopping work, leaving house and community behind for a destination unknown, sailing the ocean while putting my life and the lives of others on the line,

Maybe even sailing's been just a metaphor all along; the real journey toward wholeness is, for each of us, an inside job.

and loving another imperfect being. All that in pursuit of a more in-depth, engaged life.

I sailed into the emptiness only to discover that life is not about resolution; we just keep adding capacity to engage more of the mystery.

And *that* is the miracle.

Sunset in Florida

EPILOGUE

Perhaps my father said it best when referring to his failing vision. "I've lost so much already; if they now take away my ability to drive, I won't have much to live for." The power of his statement still haunts me today, almost seventeen years later.

Dad was near the end of his life. He was only seventy-three years old, but had suffered the pain of gradually losing his ability to engage in a wide spectrum of activities. Much of what he took for granted in his midlife, and assumed he would engage in during his later years, became just a painful memory.

Hardening of the arteries had him abstaining from walks on the beach with Mother, and an uncontrollable shaking of his hands put an end to his building and flying of model airplanes, a cherished hobby since childhood. While sitting on the outdoor patio with my mother, I watched him walk with a hint of resignation toward the waiting car that would drive him to the optometrist. Little did I know that this would be the last time I would see him alive, or that his parting statement about driving, deprivation, and death would be both prophetic for him, and an advance notice for me.

And so it is with all of us. No one is spared the pain of loss during the final third of our lives. Capacities diminish and things fail, plain and simple. My mother was, and still is fond of saying (with a wry smile on her face), "Don't get old," as if progressing in age were something we had any control over. Her smile when delivering this message to her four sons diminishes as each year passes. Years ago it was funny. Now the poignancy of it has more weight than levity.

A first glimpse into my own process of aging came one day when Evan, my fourteen-year-old son, and I, were out for a recreational run. As far back as my memory extends, I always adjusted my pace so that we would meet the finish line together. Not that day. At only fifty-six, I struggled to keep up with this growing boy who seemed to effortlessly leap ahead of me, leaving an aging man behind to huff and puff.

Similarly, our tennis matches always ended with roughly the same close outcome. Then, one day, instead of fixing the result, I unexpectedly had to embrace defeat. I said to Evan after he triumphantly walked off the tennis court, "So, did you ever wonder why the score in our tennis matches remained the same over all these years? Do you think maybe you could gently, and in a not-too-obvious fashion, continue that trend?" He didn't respond, but the silence was deafening. No controlling the outcome anymore; moving forward it would need to be more a matter of acceptance, and the transition hasn't been easy.

As if to reinforce the message, my cousin Jeff approached me a few months later at my father's funeral and said, with a gesture toward the casket, "Well Ed, we're next." Sure made me stop and pause. Embedded in the inference was the fact that my father was the last of the previous generation, and that cousin Jeff and I would likely be the next in our family lineage to meet this same fate head-on. His terse remark also said to me, "Okay, this is it; we're on the last stretch, so make it count." But making it count while capacities are failing can be quite challenging, even when not engaged in a comparison with your much-younger son.

Relatively speaking, I'm still in pretty good shape for someone in his mid-sixties. I can usually engage pain-free in physical activities like swimming, biking, and walking; appear reasonably coherent; and even engage in amorous activities without concern that the plumbing won't function properly—well, most of the time. But does the picture look like it did in my forties, or even my fifties? Due to nerve damage from an otherwise successful back surgery several years ago, I can no longer run with ease. My walk is with a slight and—to me—embarrassing limp. Tennis with Evan is a distant memory. Those things we call "senior moments" continue to increase in frequency. And forget about keeping up with the whirl of technological advances, which left me in the dust many years ago.

How does it feel? In truth, sometimes I can integrate the advancing limitations quite gracefully, and other times not so much. There is no doubt that the trajectory is a slow and steady decline, and no matter how fast I paddle, the physical capacity race is not one I can win. Sometimes I feel grateful for what I have, and at other times downright frustrated for what I don't. But from deep within there is also a growing sense of acceptance that helps to soften me and diminish the angst inside. On a good day it even feels like I'm gaining on things; that the turbulence of transition into the final third of my life has begun to dampen. *So, what has made the difference?*

Over time I've come to understand that it is all a matter of identity. Who am I? Or more to the point, who do I think I am? If I think I am only my physical body, the rest of my life will be experienced as a decline, as a loss. If, however, I experience myself primarily as a spiritual being in a human body, the picture begins to change, or is assisted by the wisdom of advancing years. After all, would a gardener think he was his hoe, or a painter her paintbrush? Then why should we think we are just our physical bodies, or even just our personalities?

My self-imposed suffering turns out to be simply a case of mistaken identity, a symptom that emerges when I too strongly identify with my physical form—the one that continues to deteriorate year after year. If, instead, I choose to move beyond the limitations of a falsely imposed identity, and accept my connection with all that is, even embrace that *I am all that is*, then the entire cosmos opens to me. I begin to experience life as a continuous opening, rather than as a gradual closing. That the older I get, the more connected and the more expansive I feel.

Over time I have grown to embrace the truth—that we are pure light, pure energy, and pure love. While I may not be able to live from that place all of the time, even connecting to it on occasion has been transformative. Gradually I've become less constrained by the weightiness of my physical and emotional structure (however beautiful and fun-filled they may seem at times). Now I am more awake to the eternal, to the place prior to form and, most importantly, to the understanding that *I am that place.*

I'm reminded of a friend's favorite response when I get on my soapbox and deliver some of this spiritual advice to him. "Well Ed [yawning], call me when you have it down." And he has a point. This wholesale change in perception doesn't come as fast or as easily as trying on new shoes. I have found that it is a very challenging and slow-paced shift in how I perceive my place in the world.

But the good news is that this alteration in how I see myself—connecting to the blissful truth of whom I really am—has the power to change my experience of aging from a sense of loss, to a sense of gain. It has allowed me to gradually encounter the remaining chapters as an act of grace, and to embrace this life transition as a major leap forward in my expanding capacity as a loving, spiritual being.

This Getting Old

It's a good thing we wait until last to get old
The final act requires our greatest skill and attention
But lest we think there is work to be done
It's harder—only surrender and letting go.

Ed Merck, 2010

OVER SIXTY

These are the salad days,
these are the days when the rivers
rejoice on entering the ocean.
We wear T-shirts
and slip-ons for our feet.
We THINK polka.
We awaken steeped in sex.
Our friends wait for us
in the dreams we drift back into.
We are not forgetful,
we just have no interest in the dust
that hovers and stifles.
Dust shall not obscure
the twinkle in an eye
nor a glimpse of beauty.
Dust shall not clog
our whistling words
when everyone is our friend.
The train we are on
is picking up speed
after the long plains.
It eats the valleys and mountains.
Up ahead gleams the Pacific,
which we approach with a certain hilarity.

Eric Nisula, 2008

ACKNOWLEDGEMENTS

In the end it all remains a mystery, especially that we appear to *know* nothing, yet *are* everything. Attempts by us to make things "knowable" seem feeble, and often destructive. But we do have each other to provide support and comfort along the journey. For that I am grateful.

The manifestation of *Sailing the Mystery* was made possible only as a result of guidance and inspiration from many quarters of my life. Cited below, with gratitude, is the list of friends, colleagues, and advisors I would like to thank publicly. Likely there are some I have forgotten. More likely, I have understated the importance of those here acknowledged. My sincere apology, and gratitude to both.

Charlotte Rodziewicz, my first editor and enthusiastic cheerleader

Kendall Dudley, astute, persistent, and imaginative editor

Dori Mintzer, reader, who added context and the other gender's view

Alan O'Hare, whose abundant inspiration even found its way into the book's title

Ruth Mullen, a tireless friend, who provided constant and empathic feedback, a place to work, and a ready heart

Son Evan, Mother Sabina, Father Edwin, and brothers Tom, John, and Michael, all of whom made this book, and my life, possible and worth living

Megan Radford, freelance editor, for her perceptive editing

Rob Sheeran, designer of the book's cover, Website, and most stylistic elements that permeate and enhance the book's layout design

David Caldwell, friend and technical advisor

Ellen Schaeffer, whose wonderful images gracefully introduce several chapters

Coleman Barks, for use of the passage from his translation of the Rumi poem, *"Bouyancy"*

Eric Nisula, for use of his poem, *"Over Sixty"*

Faith Wilbur, Peter D'Alessandro, Frank and Holly DiMauro, for warm cozy places to write

Leah Chyten, for sharing her deep insights

Kathie Allen, Account Manager from FriesenPress, for her steadying presence throughout all the surprising (to me) twists and turns of transforming a manuscript into a book

Colin Parks, Senior Designer from FriesenPress, who generously, and patiently, applied his abundant skills throughout the process

Cynthia Bloomquist, who helped with the unenviable task of cleaning up my writing at the eleventh hour

Kathy and Denise...

Spirit, who wrote this book (at least the better sections of it)

Ed Merck, May 2013

ABOUT THE AUTHOR

Ed Merck spent thirty rewarding years as chief financial officer and/or a member of the music faculty at several prestigious universities and colleges. Subsequently, as an entrepreneur, Ed co-developed Future Perfect, the premier computer-based strategic/financial planning model used in higher education today. In recent years, Ed has gravitated towards pursuits of the heart—writing, making music, teaching yoga, and offering workshops on "Conscious Aging." He currently resides on Martha's Vineyard, Massachusetts, and can be reached at www.sailingthemystery.com

CPSIA information can be obtained
at www.ICGtesting.com
Printed in the USA
BVOW03s0904151017
497709BV00001B/100/P